Making Sense of the Events
That Changed Our World

Why were the World Trade Center and the Pentagon attacked on September 11, 2001? Why do terrorists do what they do? Why now? How will our economy be affected? What will happen to international relationships? What can we expect in the future?

Since 1901, Llewellyn has published valuable astrological books and resources for astrologers and non-astrologers alike. We asked a group of seven professional astrologers to explore the tragic events of September 11, the indicators that could have predicted the attack, and the historical and political underpinnings of the new global threat.

Using the techniques of astrology, the only science that allows us to examine a specific moment in time, the authors of this book offer us some answers to the difficult questions we face in these turbulent times.

D0171665

About the Editor

A professional astrologer for over twenty-five years, Stephanie Jean Clement, Ph.D., is a board member of the American Federation of Astrologers and a faculty member of Kepler College. Her Ph.D. in Transpersonal Psychology has prepared her to work with clients in defining their creative potential and refining their creative process. Her published books include *Charting Your Career; Dreams: Working Interactive, What Astrology Can Do for You; The Power of the Midheaven*; and *Charting Your Spiritual Path with Astrology* is due out soon.

To Write to the Editor

If you wish to contact the editor or would like more information about this book, please write to the editor in care of Llewellyn Worldwide and we will forward your request. Both the author and publisher appreciate hearing from you and learning of your enjoyment of this book and how it has helped you. Llewellyn Worldwide cannot guarantee that every letter written to the editor can be answered, but all will be forwarded. Please write to:

Stephanie Clement
% Llewellyn Worldwide
P.O. Box 64383, Dept. 0-7387-0247-1
St. Paul, MN 55164-0383, U.S.A.

Please enclose a self-addressed stamped envelope for reply, or $1.00 to cover costs. If outside U.S.A., enclose international postal reply coupon.

Many of Llewellyn's authors have websites with additional information and resources. For more information, please visit our website at http://www.llewellyn.com

CIVILIZATION UNDER ATTACK

SEPTEMBER 11, 2001 & BEYOND

AN ASTROLOGICAL PERSPECTIVE

Edited by Stephanie Jean Clement, Ph.D.

2001
Llewellyn Publications
St. Paul, Minnesota 55164-0383, U.S.A.

First Edition
First Printing, 2001

Cover art © 2001 Digital Stock (earth), Photodisc (banner)
Cover design by Kevin R. Brown
Editing by Sharon Leah

ISBN 0-7387-0247-1
Library of Congress Cataloging-in-Publication (Pending)

Llewellyn Publications
A Division of Llewellyn Worldwide, Ltd.
P.O. Box 64383, Dept. 0-7387-0247-1
St. Paul, MN 55164-0383, U.S.A.
www.llewellyn.com

Printed in the United States of America

*Dedicated to
the Spirit of America*

Thanks to Astrology House Auckland for producing the AstroMaps on the Janus astrology software. For information on AstroMaps and Janus please visit www.astrologyware.com

Contents

Preface

STEPHANIE CLEMENT

The newspapers, television, radio, and Internet have provided coverage and analysis since the events of September 11, 2001, took place. But there are times when we all want to find the deeper meaning behind events. We want to understand the "why" of things that happen to us and around us. It is our intention to offer a different perspective on the events, the people, and the decisions that led up to the attacks, and in the process, we hope to answer some questions that have risen since September 11. We recognize that our readers are intelligent, thoughtful people from countries around the world, who understand there are limitations on the information the news media can provide in the two-to three-minute news bites from television and radio reports.

To that end, Llewellyn asked a group of professional astrologers to explore the indicators that could have predicted the attack, and share their insights and offer reasonable answers to some of the questions before us. These individuals have studied the science of astrology deeply. Their experience averages nearly thirty years' study in different areas of the field of astrology. Our objective is to interpret the astrology of the people and the times by demonstrating, through the use of historical examples and, where appropriate, current events, to create a context for you, our reader, to gain better understanding.

We have avoided using astrological terms whenever possible, but for those of you who want more, the astrological information has been placed in footnotes. The astrological calculations used in writing this book have come from sophisticated computer programs, and have been carefully checked for accuracy. In instances where precise birth times of individuals and times of significant events are not known, we have included statements about why a particular chart or time was chosen.

Llewellyn and the authors have provided factual information and astrological insight into the larger meaning of the facts. This tragedy marks a turning point in our lives and our history.

In the early moments of the twenty-first century, we seek greater understanding of the needs of our planet Earth and its peoples.

Introduction

STEPHANIE CLEMENT

On September 11, 2001, four hijacked commercial flights crashed into three targets (the fourth crashed in rural Pennsylvania). Based on the takeoff time of the first hijacked plane, American Flight 11 at 7:58 A.M., astrologers can identify several important things about the events and people involved. See Figure 1 on page 239. By studying the placement of planets in the chart for the event and the symbolism of the various planets, we can discern the following:

- The hijackers had an obsessive need to complete their missions;
- The origins of the hijackers and their leaders;
- The reasons why the terrorists chose to attack the World Trade Center;
- The reasons why the second two planes didn't accomplish their missions;
- There was an immense power behind the attacks;

3

- The hijackers had a small window of opportunity that passed; and

- There will be consequences for terrorists.

Imagine, if you can, the mind of the hijacker. He had planned for months, or maybe years, to carry out the mission of his organization. Airline schedules were studied, and great care was taken to keep the plans secret. He was on a religious mission and believed that he would enter heaven the instant the plane crashed because his mission was holy. He was obsessed with his mission—he had to be, or he would have faltered and failed.[1] In the last minutes before his own death, he most assuredly said his final prayers.

By looking at the planetary aspects of Pluto in Sagittarius and Saturn in Gemini, astrologers can identify the terrorists and their religious obsession. These two planets represent many other aspects of the disastrous events, and we will discuss them in this book as well.

We also suspect that within the first minutes after Flight 175 took off, the intensity of the terrorist's obsession began to wane. The hijackers had time to think, the initial adrenaline rush began to subside, and with each passing minute the intense focus of the hijackers began to diffuse. We see this represented by the fact that the relationship between the Moon and Pluto changed immediately.

---

1. The closest astrological relationship (aspect) in this chart was between the Moon and Pluto. They were exactly 165 degrees apart on the sky. Within one minute of clock time, the aspect was complete, and the two planets began to separate from each other.

The planets did not move forward an appreciable distance in the zodiac in the time between the first and second attacks on the twin towers. What did change, however, was the astrological relationship of the Moon and Pluto to the highest point in the chart, the Midheaven (the name astrologers give to the part of the zodiac that is highest in the sky at a particular time). By the time of the second attack, Mars was in closest aspect to the Midheaven. That aspect was exact only seconds before the first plane crashed into the North Tower of the World Trade Center.[2] Astrologically, this combination indicates a condition of obsessive focus on the energy being used. It also incorporates thoughts about one's career goals. Finally, it involves the confidence we have when we are doing something we care about passionately.

The immense energy behind the attacks came from two sources. The first source was the religious zeal of the terrorists. The second, and the most powerful, source of energy was the aircraft carrying full loads of jet fuel. Each of these jets carried up to 23,000 gallons of fuel, and weighed approximately 400,000 pounds.[3] Compare this to the 35,000 pounds maximum weight and 670 gallons of fuel[4] carried on the B-25 that crashed into the Empire State Building on

---

2. The closest astrological relationship (aspect) in the chart was between Mars and the Midheaven (the part of the zodiac that was highest in the sky at the time). Mars and the Midheaven were exactly 165 degrees apart in the heavens.

3. Online at www.boeing.com/commercial/767-300/product.html; link to October 7, 2001.

4. Online at "North American B-25 Mitchell," at www.csd.uwo.ca/~pet-typi/ elevon/baugher_us.

July 25, 1945.[5] That crash caused about $1,000,000 in damage, and did not destroy the structural integrity of the building. So each of the jets crashed by terrorists carried about thirty-five times as much fuel, and weighed about twelve times as much as a B-25.

The second pair of planes was different. They did not reach the intended targets—at least we can be certain that the Pennsylvania crash plane did not. What were the hijackers thinking? They probably believed they would still go straight to heaven, but they knew they were going to die, having failed in their missions. The obsession of the task (as shown in the planetary alignments in the charts for these events) had time to wear down, and be replaced by doubt. Fear may have replaced obsession. As the optimum moment for the terrorist attack receded into the past, even by a few minutes, the outcomes changed dramatically.

America Strikes Back

After waiting nearly a month to consider strategy and develop a coalition of international support, the United States attacked terrorist targets in Afghanistan.[6] On October 7, 2001, the United States, in concert with its allies around the world, attacked terrorist bases southwest of Kabul, Afghanistan, and also the headquarters of the ruling Taliban militia in Kandahar. This attack began at 8:57 P.M. Afghanistan

---

5. Available online at www.greatbuildings.com, and at www.esbnyc.com, September 23, 2001.

6. Associated Press report at www.dailynews.yahoo.com, October 7, 2001.

time, or 12:27 P.M. in Washington D.C. The half-hour time difference in time occurs because Afghanistan sets its time to be four-and-one-half hours later than Greenwich time, while most of the world uses even-hour time differences.

In the October 7 chart for the attack on Osama bin Laden's organized terrorists in Afghanistan, there are two relationships (aspects) of the same kind as we have been discussing. The first depicts the obsessive energy we have invested in our associations with our allies during the past few weeks. The second indicates that we are also obsessed with resolving the terrorist problems in the world, and that we are doing this with the full cooperation of our allies around the world. The big astrological difference is that this pattern will not go away in a few minutes. The relationship is moving into exactness. Using normal astrological methods, we can conclude that this aspect will be in force until at least November 2, and possibly until December 9, 2001.[7]

The president, in his speech to the world on October 7, indicated that along with the military strikes, the government was also airlifting desperately needed food and supplies to the Afghan people. He made the statement that this is not a war against Afghanistan, but against terrorism. As

---

7. The quindecile of Pluto and the North Node is moving into exactness, and will take a long time: Transiting Pluto completes the aspect to the Node in this chart on November 2, 2001, while the transiting Node completes the aspect to Pluto in this chart on December 9, 2001. Even after waiting nearly a month to take action, time has not run out on the United States and its allies.

events unfold over the next months and years, we will see if the United States has taken a step toward reducing terrorism and increasing peaceful relationships among nations.

In this book, we offer the opinions of prominent astrologers. Each discusses the events and their future meanings from a different perspective. As events unfold, we will see how our analysis meshes with the events. We hope you will find this information worth serious consideration. The demands of writing for different audiences, with different purposes, on different subjects create variables that cannot be anticipated in a book like this, and we recognize that. We have attempted to avoid ambiguity, so as not to leave our words open to misinterpretation.

Attack on America

Jonathan Keyes

On the morning of September 11, 2001, at approximately 8:46 A.M., American Flight 11, carrying ninety-two people, crashed into the upper floors of the World Trade Center North Tower. At 9:03 A.M., United Flight 175, carrying sixty-five people, crashed into the South Tower. At 9:43 A.M., as people in the twin towers scrambled toward safety, United Flight 77, carrying sixty-four people, crashed into the Pentagon building. A fourth plane, United Flight 93, carrying forty-five people, crashed into a field in western Pennsylvania at about 10:10 A.M. In addition to those who died in the plane crashes, 126 people died in the Pentagon, and more than 4,700 people are missing and presumed dead in the World Trade Center buildings.

A Loss of Innocence

When the second plane crashed into the World Trade Center, it became clear that the United States was under attack. As details about the attacks were revealed and we learned that nineteen hijackers had commandeered the four planes, a massive investigation that spanned the globe was initiated. While only three of the hijackers are known to have direct ties to terrorist leader Osama bin Laden, at the time of this printing, it is believed that all of the hijackers had ties to al Qaida, bin Laden's terrorist organization. Bin Laden, an exiled, militant Saudi Arabian, is reportedly living in the hills of Afghanistan under the protection of the Taliban, a fundamentalist Islamic group.

In his address before the joint session of Congress and the world on September 20, President George W. Bush said, "On September 11, enemies of freedom committed an act of war against our country. . . . Our war on terror begins with al Qaida, but it does not end there."[1]

We are at a turning point in the history of the world as we know it. The brutal attacks on the cities and people of the United States mark the beginning of a new world order.

An Astrological Perspective

To gain understanding about what was happening on the day of the attack, astrologers look to the planets for information. Two planets in particular, Saturn and Pluto, stand out as being significant because of their alignment,[2] and

---

1. The complete text from President Bush's speech on September 20, 2001, is available online at www.whitehouse.gov.

2. Saturn in Gemini and Pluto in Sagittarius are forming an opposition (180 degrees apart). An opposition brings to focus things having to do with perspective—how we view things, and how we balance things. The events that are physical representations of astrological occurrences—the attacks, for example—represent two sides of the same core issue, but from totally different ends of the spectrum. Astrologers will look at the signs (Gemini and Sagittarius), the aspects, and the placement of each planet in a house, for information.

because they represent very powerful forces. These two planets began moving into opposition with each other (meaning they are located in opposite parts of the sky) in July 2001. Oppositions of planets such as these often indicate difficult times of intense challenges. As we look at the symbolism of these two planets, astrologers see planetary alignments with powerful potential that proved to be a pivotal time for in the history of the United States and the world.[3]

Four areas of life that Saturn is representative of are:

- Structure: the foundations and formations that we build on both a psychological and material level;

- Authority: the authority we have over ourselves, and external authority of others over us;

- Discipline: the disciple to the cause, and the discipline to abide by limitations; and

- Commerce: the buildings and businesses that comprise our economy.

At this time, Saturn is moving through the sign of Gemini. Gemini, an air sign, is commonly associated with communication, and local, as opposed to long-distance, travel. Gemini is also known as the sign of the twins.[4] In the event chart for the time of the first plane crash, Saturn (commerce) was in the sector of the chart that represents foreign affairs, law, justice, philosophy, morals, and so on. See Figure 2 on page 240.

---

3. See Robert Hand, "Putting Events on the World Map," in this book for additional information about locating trouble spots in the world.

4. See Stephanie Clement, "'Twin Events," in this book for a more complete discussion of the twin symbolism of Gemini.

Pluto is representative of deep, all-encompassing trans-formation, which can be experienced as a physical, emo-tional, or spiritual death. It is associated with dark, destruc-tive forces and abuse of power. The attacks, believed to have been perpetrated by militant, fundamentalist Muslims, are one such expression of Pluto's dark expression of power.

Pluto is transiting through the sign of Sagittarius. As planets transit through a sign, the energy on the Earth changes to bring into focus those things symbolized by the sign the planet is in. Sagittarius is a fiery sign that is associ-ated with belief systems, law, teaching, and religion, among other things. This is therefore a time when the violent and vengeful aspects of religious traditions are rising.

This Pluto transit signifies a powerful shift in conscious-ness that will address relationships and communication be-tween the Western world and the Arab world. The terrorists struck at the very core of our beliefs about war, peace, and justice.[5] Since the attacks we have had to change how citi-zens travel, how we secure our borders, and how we treat others of different religious faiths.

Transits of Pluto can often start out destructively, but the destruction is followed by rebuilding and greater wis-dom. Perhaps, in time, the World Trade Centers will be re-built, or a monument will be built in its place to memorial-ize the people who died there.

Millions of us witnessed the destruction of the World Trade Center towers, as well as an attack on the Pentagon

---

5. Astrologically, this is expressed through Saturn in Gemini opposing Pluto in Sagittarius.

through images broadcast on televisions. Citizens of this country, and countries around the world, have experienced a deep psychological wound that will take time to heal. On a deeper level, the foundation of the United States has been damaged and will require time to rebuild. Though the alignment of Saturn and Pluto did not cause events such as this to happen, astrologers throughout the ages have witnessed that alignments such as these often manifest as pivotal events in our history.

Previous Pluto-Saturn Opposition and Its Implication

The last time that Saturn and Pluto made an opposition was from April 23, 1965, to February 20, 1966. Saturn was passing through the sign of Pisces, while Pluto was in the sign of Virgo. Although that alignment took place in different signs from where it is now occurring, that, too, was a time of transformation and upheaval across the globe. It was during those years that Americans witnessed our involvement with Vietnam widen, race riots erupted in major cities across the country and the conflict in the Middle East was growing.

As tensions mounted, Israel launched attacks on June 5, 1967, against Syria, Egypt, and Iraq, to protect their lands. The Six-Day War[6] resulted in the West Bank and the Golan Heights being taken. Certainly, the Six-Day War is, in part, responsible for some of the emotion behind the conflicts

---

6. For more information about the Six-Day War see www.hsje.org/six_day_war.htm.

that are taking place now. One of the reasons that bin Laden lists for attacking America has to do with Israel's occupation of the lands where about 1.2 million Arabs live.[7] As Saturn and Pluto come back to oppose each other, the issues and tensions that surrounded that initial war are coming back to the surface.[8]

Recommended Reading

1949, The First Israelis by Tom Segev and Arlen Neal Weinstein (Henry Holt: April 1998).

The Birth of the Palestinian Refugee Problem, 1947–1949 by Benny Morris (Cambridge University Press: April 1989).

---

7. Jonathan Tilove, "Exploring the Arab World," Newhouse News Services (*Oregonian*, September 21, 2001), A6.
8. See Robert Hand, *"Where Do We Go From Here?"*, in this book for more discussion of what is known about the cycles of planets and events.

The Psychology of Terrorism

BERNIE ASHMAN

I was a child in the 1950s, during the Cold War, but the collective fear of a nuclear attack remains a vivid memory. There was a drill called "duck and cover" where we had to get under our school desks or kneel down in a hallway and duck our heads as though we were being bombed. The concern in my parent's faces during the Cuban Missile Crisis in 1962, when John F. Kennedy was president of the United States, was a portrait of sorrow. They worried that the world, as they knew it, could come to an end.

But the fear I've seen in many people's faces due to the recent terrorist attacks at the World Trade Center in Manhattan, and at the Pentagon, in Washington, D.C., surpasses the fear we experienced then. At least we knew the identity of our enemy during the Cold War. But terrorists operate in the shadows, and, often after an attack, nobody is certain of the perpetrators identities. The fear we feel today is fear with an eerie mystique.

Terrorists intend to leave permanent scars, and to keep us scared until the next attack. The idea is to disrupt our sense of security, leaving us in a constant state of anxiety. A terrorist has only one thing in mind and he or she will use any means to justify the end. They hope the fallout of their dark deeds—post-traumatic stress—will continue to escalate, bringing everyday business and daily routines of the targeted group to a screeching halt.

The September 11 attacks struck at two strong symbols of American society: our financial district and our military power. The terrorist's goal is to belittle the symbolic meaning of our institutions, and to destroy the faith of the people sharing in its belief.

Is There a Predictable Terrorist Mind?

The experts answer with an emphatic "No!" A terrorist can be well educated or have no formal education. He or she can be rich or poor; or a sophisticated world traveler, as we have witnessed. So, if there is no precise psychological type, what is a common ingredient? A terrorist will sacrifice personal will to a group that is usually controlled by a charismatic, or fanatical, leader, to support the common cause. Individuality is sacrificed to the group plan. Therefore, the next step to understanding the psychology of terrorism is to glimpse into the mind of one of its leaders, Osama bin Laden.

Osama bin Laden

Osama bin Laden has been credited to be the primary architect behind the recent assault on the United States. His exact date and time of birth are not known. The only reliable information is that he was born in 1957. But this alone reveals much about what drives him on this campaign of terror.

The following statements about bin Laden's astrological influences do not apply to everyone born in 1957. For, while most of the people born that year have astrological influences similar to bin Laden's, the majority made more appropriate choices in acting out their destinies.

It is important to note here that contemporary astrologers do not believe that planets do anything to people, nor do they cause events to happen here on Earth. We do believe, based on thousands of years of observation, that planets and the relationships that form between them— mathematical alignments, including, but not exclusively— squares with 90 degrees separation between planets, trines with 120 degrees separation, and so on—reflect information about events and people here on Earth. The planet in astrology that most represents ambition and leadership is Saturn. In 1957, Saturn was in the sign of Sagittarius.

There are many things associated with the sign Sagittarius. Among them are: a desire for freedom and independence; a love for law and religion; an interest in the world—foreign lands and people, in particular; and a love of horses and for hunting. People with strong Sagittarius influence in their lives are often drawn to careers in teaching, law, or religion. They can be very idealistic, as well. Bin Laden has made it his mission to recruit followers to his cause, which is to defeat the "corrupted" Western world. He preaches death and pledges a jihad, or holy war, to those who would oppose him. This man, projecting a zeal for a new and radical interpretation of Islam as the way to battle the enemies of the Western world, has packaged his message in religious dogma. His extremism captures individuals in search of a mission, but unable to create a more authentic one of their own.

There are other indications in the astrological planetary placements of 1957 that show how bin Laden got off track. Planetary alignments indicate that certain individuals born that year could purposely lead others astray in the name of a false ideal.[1] Reality-orientation is not one of bin Laden's strong cards to play. I don't mean in the sense of mental illness, but, more so, that he ignores the reality that there are limits to his ability to carry out his mission.[2]

---

1. In 1957, there was a square in intense alignment of 90 degrees separation between Uranus in the sign Leo and Neptune in the sign Scorpio. This denotes a conflict or challenge as the two planetary influences struggle to be expressed. Uranus is associated with individuality and sudden changes; Neptune is associated with idealism. The tension between the two can be resolved by establishing realistic goals. While a strong Uranus influence is usually seen in individuals with inventive tendencies, this influence can also result in eccentric—way out of mainstream—thinking. When this is combined with Neptune's propensity for idealism, or feeling that one must be the savior of a people or cause, can produce an out of control visionary. The world is also aware that Osama bin Laden could die fighting and become a martyr of the fundamentalist cause.

2. Saturn, associated with reality and limits, is put to the test in the sign Sagittarius, which is associated with breaking limitations and expanding into the world. When Saturn and Sagittarius are in harmony, wisdom and philosophy can do wonderful things together. Bin Laden has chosen to pervert, according to the worldview of most individuals, the wisdom and strength that are his birthright.

Bin Laden has a serious drive to define himself through his philosophical beliefs. Sagittarius at its best denotes tolerance, generosity, and wisdom. At its worst, this sign can be expressed as dogmatic and ruthless, and intolerant in their judgment of others.

Saturn can also be expressed as wisdom, and as purposeful limitations. However, this planetary symbolism also encompasses the dysfunctional role of rigidity, and holding onto strict interpretations of traditions—as in strict fundamentalism.

In order for bin Laden and others like him to accomplish their goals, however, they must have followers. Extremism captures individuals, in search of a mission, whom will follow in their leader's footsteps. The orientation of such individuals points to problems with low self-esteem, as we see in American culture among people who affiliate themselves with gangs. Members are encouraged not to think for themselves, and to adhere to the group ideology.

Anatomy of a Terrorist Mind

Astrologers study a birth chart,[3] like a driver studies a road map, for information. Planets in their signs at the time of a birth are symbolic of how that event or individual will potentially experience life. When the chart is properly interpreted, it yields useful information that an individual can use as a tool on the path of self-discovery. Astrology recognizes

---

3. Astrologers use the exact time, date, and place of birth to erect an individual birth chart for a person or an event. The planetary symbols and aspects are the astrologers "blueprint" or "map," that is used for interpretation of the birth or event.

that there are no guarantees, and that some individuals will choose the shadow over the light. Each of us has to choose the directions that are best for us.

The following analysis of the planets is intended as a guide to show how each of us can become part of the terrorist thinking. Think of it as a blueprint of the terrorist psyche. Let me please emphasize that these descriptions are focused on what happens when someone gets lost in the darkness, or shadow, of what these symbolic planets truly represent.

The Sun: The Life Force

The Sun in astrology symbolizes the individual ego—the basic part of self-expression that must shine in its own way. Each of us wants to be a hero in our own right and the ego supports that effort. What happens to this key part of one's identity if it is surrendered to an extremist mentality? Instead of an authentic development of ego strength, a terrorist is essentially deriving all of his or her sense of self through what the leader or group deems as important. Personal will power, another theme of the Sun, merges with the will of the particular ideology. This can take the form of hijacking a plane, or whatever role as determined by the leader. But what you really have is a person at the mercy of whoever has taken over piloting his or her life.

The ego will, however, resist any attempts to make it what it is not by acting with greater intensity until its true nature cannot be denied.[4] So, with time, the terrorist becomes more dangerous.

---

4. See Kevin Burk, *Understanding the Birth Chart*, (Llewellyn, 2000).

The Moon: Creator of Security and Belonging

The Moon symbolizes the quest for security, how an individual expresses and receives nurturing, and the need for a home. The terrorist's sense of belonging, or intimacy, is obtained from the movement or the cause he or she is devoted to; comfort is obtained through those assisting their actions in the form of food and shelter; and home is wherever they are currently living in hiding. The terrorist, in turn, nurtures the goal.

Mercury: The Messenger

Mercury is symbolic of the thinking process and how information is gathered. In the mind of the terrorist, communication is crucial to the relay of important details in an operation. The mindset of terrorism is conditioned completely by the education of the group mentality. When feelings are objectively nullified, and brainwashing is so thorough that one's mind stops analyzing in rational terms, it makes doing damage that much easier for a terrorist. The logic of killing and doing harm fits into the teachings of the group cause.

Venus: Attraction to Values and Relationships

Venus is symbolic of social instincts, peers, and relationships. Terrorists are hard to detect because they stay close-knit in their own organizations, they are hard to detect. They do not reveal much about themselves to anyone but their own clan. Terrorists only value what will help them accomplish their desired aims. Their value system is inflexible and focuses on creating chaos and destruction for their targeted populations of people. Physical pleasures and appetites are part of Venus symbolism, and bin Laden has sold his followers on the idea of suicide bombings by saying there will be plenty of sensual gratification and other rewards in the next life.

Mars: Warrior of the World

Mars is often associated with aggression and self-centeredness—warrior qualities. While most of us are planning how to be assertive, the terrorist is using aggressive tactics to obtain his or her goals. Another side of aggression is anger. The terrorist will select the most dreadful weapon, or destroy a target, the destruction of which will take away our air, and ultimately our hope. One theory suggests that some terrorists are taught as children to hate anything associated with Western culture, and terrorist groups manipulate this ingrained hatred, turning individuals into trained assassins.

Jupiter: Philosopher, Lawyer, Teacher

Jupiter is representative of philosophy, religion, law, learning, teaching, and foreign or long-distance travel. It is also connected to experiences that are foreign (even exporting terrorism to other countries). Terrorists accept a dogmatic view of the world, and ridding the world of those not believing in their way is felt as a duty. Instead of the natural openness, morality is translated into a bankrupt sense of right and wrong in the hands of terrorism. People with belief systems that differ from their own are dismissed, or lumped together and labeled as the enemy. The religious overtones of Jupiter are conveniently put into an oversimplified formula by bin Laden and others like him.

Saturn: Master of Time and Structure

As stated earlier, Saturn is associated with ambition. It is also associated with restriction, authority, control, and structure. Bin Laden's organization, al Qaida, is a highly bureaucratic organization with a well-defined hierarchy. Terrorists, organized into small groups known as cells, are deployed around the world. Each cell is assigned a specific function. The members are bonded together in the cause. It's so tight that different cell groups can participate in an attack and yet never know who one another is because each moves into action at well-organized times. The terrorists' fanatical way of viewing the world is what sets the tone for violence, from top to bottom. Terrorist organizations with an ambitious leader like bin Laden want power. They may not be openly saying this but it's definitely part of their scheme.

Uranus: Creative Inspiration and Destroyer

Uranus symbolizes uniqueness, originality, rebellion, and destruction, among other things. Whereas the leader of terrorist organizations may express creative inspiration, originality, and have a gift for doing the unexpected, those who follow him sacrifice individuality to the goals of the group. They are easy to train because they are not interested in seeking their own paths. Also, this planet is said to denote one's opinions about groups. Understanding this makes it easier to comprehend a terrorist's allegiance to the future of the group above all else.

Neptune: Idealism, Faith, and Delusion

Neptune is associated with ideals, romanticism, compassion, and faith. A terrorist demonstrates these qualities by following a leader in blind faith. This is only possible when someone surrenders their own ideals to follow a misguided cause. Most people would feel guilt (another Neptune characteristic) about committing hideous acts against humanity. Why don't terrorists feel guilt? Because they make use of another Neptune trait—denial. There is no guilt when you believe you are right and serving the highest cause as determined by your leader.

Pluto: Ultimate Destructive Force in the Universe

Pluto is associated with power, passion, self-mastery, and secrecy.[5] In terrorism, this energy becomes fanaticism. The passion to destroy and kill—assassinate—in the name of crazed beliefs, is justified in the terrorists' mind. Terrorists hide in the shadows and work in underground networks.[6] But even though one of Pluto's associations is death (destruction), Pluto is also about rebirth. So a victim of such an attack—survivors and American citizens—can recover very powerfully!

---

5. Pluto can symbolize projecting one's hatred onto others, whether individually, or in a collective manner as in the events of September 11, 2001.

6. Pluto also represents money systems. It is a known fact that terrorist organizations have covert ways of hiding their financial sources. It is also interesting to note that in the chart erected for the first attack on the World Trade Center Towers, transiting Pluto is in opposition (180 degrees apart) to the placement of Pluto in the charts for Manhattan and New York City. Carolyn Dodson, in her book *Horoscopes of the U.S. and Cities* (ACS Publications, 1985), lists the Manhattan chart as February 12, 1653, and New York City (based on the consolidation of the five boroughs) as January 1, 1892.

The George W. Bush Chart

JONATHAN KEYES

To understand the underpinnings of the recent attacks from an astrological perspective, it is helpful to look at the birth chart of the United States.[1] From that chart, the first thing that becomes noticeable is that the current Saturn/Pluto opposition is crossing over the Ascendant and Descendant of the United States chart. See Figure 13 on page 251. This astrological "signature" indicates that how the rest of the world sees the United States and how we as a people are responding and acting in the world is undergoing a massive transformation that at times could be somewhat intense and difficult.

Another important chart to examine in this whole tragedy is the chart of President George W. Bush. Bush's role in this conflict is of paramount concern because he

---

1. The Declaration of Independence was given at 5:10 P.M., 1776, in Philadelphia, Pennsylvania, and that is the chart I use here. There are other charts for the United States, but I have chosen this one because it seems to be the most accurate.

makes some of the final decisions. As commander in chief of the armed forces, Bush chooses when, where, and how he may want to direct this conflict. Because a massive attack has been leveled at the United States, congressional support is not required before Bush can order our military forces to retaliate, although he has chosen to seek their support along with international support for his aims. See Figure 5 on page 243.

When looking at his chart, we see a few key factors. Although George W. Bush's Sun is in Cancer, his chart is strongly accented by the sign of Leo.[2] Leo is symbolic of courage, expressiveness, charm, and generosity. But the darker side of Leo is selfish, kingly, and arrogant. For example, Bush demonstrated his charming side to cameras and the American public during the early days of the vote recount in November 2000. But when the decision was delayed for several weeks, Bush's kingly, arrogant side began to show. There is no doubt that this is a man who can be intense, tenacious, and wrathful when angered.[3] On the other side, it shows someone who is willing to stand up and fight, to be strong and almost obsessive in meeting his goals. Although public approval is extremely important to individuals with strong Leo in their chart, it is unlikely that

---

2. Bush's Ascendant, Mercury, Pluto, and Venus all reside in the sign of Leo.

3. Mercury, Pluto, and the Ascendant are conjoined in Leo, signifying the temperament described. Mars in the Second House and the sign of Virgo indicates that he will feel most aggressive when something or someone threatens his security or that which he values.

he will back down from this fight, even if approval of his war actions declines.

In Bush's birth chart, Mercury is within one degree of Pluto in the zodiac. Mercury is associated with communication, Pluto with transformation, and Bush has often had difficulty in his speaking ability—choosing wrong words or mispronouncing—that has hampered his effectiveness as a leader and caused him numerous problems. Bush's choice of words when interacting with the global community is of paramount concern in these times for the wrong words can have the effect of angering or even galvanizing opposing forces.

Bush has a Libra Moon that is within two degrees of being conjunct Jupiter, also in Libra. This Moon/Jupiter pair lends him charm and grace, and helps him to build coalitions.[4] He will need to rely on his ability to be persuasive and community oriented to help him build and maintain the international coalition against terrorism.

Bush's Sun in Cancer shows someone who feels things strongly.[5] If you remember in his impromptu talk with reporters after speaking with Governor George Pataki and

---

4. Some conjunctions, such as the Mercury/Pluto conjunction in Bush's chart, can cause problems, however, the Moon/Jupiter conjunction in Libra is beneficial. Whether the astrological indicator is experienced as beneficial or not is dependent on several factors, including the two planets involved and the aspects those planets make to other planets in the birth chart.

5. Bush has his Sun in Cancer in the Twelfth House. Because he has several planets in Leo along with the ascendant, his Leo side can often appear more strongly than his hidden Sun in Cancer.

Mayor Rudolph Giuliani, Bush said, "I'm a loving guy," and he choked up as tears welled up in his eyes. The attack on the United States impacted Bush on many levels, but essentially it hit him at a gut emotional level. Bush brings his emotions into his words and he should beware of taking actions strictly from this level before examining the possible implications of all his choices.

Cancer is the sign of the crab, a fierce and protective creature that can hide in its shell as well as lash out with its claws if it feels threatened. In Bush's short time as president before the attack, he mainly focused on internal policy and chose to ignore being part of a greater global community. Bush turned down signing on the Kyoto accords, which would have changed environmental policies dramatically. Bush also withdrew the government's involvement in a conference on race relations in South Africa, which interestingly sparred over the word choice of depicting Israel as racist and oppressive towards Arab peoples. Because of the recent attacks, Bush has been forced to act as an international leader and call on the support of nations throughout the world. The United States government has been forced to move away from an isolationist standpoint to one in which it is intertwined with the rest of the world.

Conclusion

In this time of great hardship and confusion, Bush has rallied the troops and talked to the American people about the need for a long and sustained war against terrorism. Bush has chosen to view this conflict as a war of "Good versus Evil," as a time to root out the "evil doers" and the states that support them. What he confronts is the possibility of inciting tremendous anger in the Arab world, and escalating the conflict into global proportions. Bush walks a fine line in this dangerous time, and it is up to him and the American people to make choices that will ensure justice, but not at the cost of a global catastrophe.

It is also a time for every citizen of the United States to examine the question: Why have we engendered so much hatred in certain sections of the world? We need to examine our approach to foreign policy, our interaction with the Arab world, and our belief that we are isolated from the rest of the world.

There is a chance for America to go through a tremendous transformation and rebirth, where the best parts about this great country survive—tolerance for religious and political differences, as well as the strength and courage exemplified by the firefighters and rescue workers who worked tirelessly to save lives.

The United States' Chart

ROBERT HAND

M ost people who have looked at astrology, even in the most casual way, know that everyone has a birth chart. This is a chart that shows schematically where all of the planets are in the zodiac and how they are related at the place and time of a specific birth. For the most part astrologers agree that the time of birth is the moment when the newborn draws his or her first breath. Some of the older astrologers give a somewhat different definition stating that the birth moment occurred when the baby was halfway out of the womb. Whatever the truth may be, the moment of birth for a human being is fairly well agreed upon.

What many people do not know is that not only do people have birth charts but so do nations. Astrologers generally agree on this. However, nations are more difficult subjects than individuals for astrology. Some nations have no clear birth moment and some have several possible birth moments. For example, when did France come into being? It emerged gradually in the early Middle Ages but no one can say for certain what was the date before which there was no France and after which there was. Some nations have come into being at definite moments. For example, prior to 1870, or thereabouts, Germany did not exist as a nation. Instead, there was a patchwork of little kingdoms, duchies, free cities, and other principalities. After the Franco-Prussian War of 1870, Wilhelm I was crowned Emperor, or Kaiser, of Germany. This would presumably give us the birth moment of Germany. The only problem is that there were several other events at about that time which could also be used to define a birth moment.

The United States should be a clear-cut case. Our nation was created more or less intentionally and it seems that it should have come into being at a definite moment. But even with the United States there is much dispute. When did our nation come into being? Was it the at beginning of the Revolutionary War? With the Declaration of Independence? With the adoption of the Articles of Confederation? With the adoption of the Constitution? Or was it at the beginning of constitutional government? Nations are not like individuals. A human is born at a given moment. Nations may come into existence in stages.

Let's look quickly at these possibilities. We can eliminate the beginning of the Revolutionary War as the moment because for about a year after the war began in 1775 most of those fighting against Britain were still fighting more for a new and reformed relationship with the mother country than for complete separation. It was not until the summer of 1776 that the delegates to the Second Continental Congress began to think that a complete separation was in order. On July 2, 1776, some time in the afternoon the Congress passed the following resolution:

> "Resolved, that these United Colonies are, and, of right ought to be, Free and Independent States: that they are absolved from all allegiance to the British crown, and that all political connection between them, and the state of Great Britain, is, and ought to be, totally dissolved." [Capitalization and punctuation as in original][1]

On July 4, 1776, at some time during the day, the Declaration was formally adopted and sent to press. July 2 or 4 is clearly the date of the beginning of the statutory independence of the colonies from Britain, at least from the American point of view. However, was it a nation at this point or a group of independent colonies? Later dates that are of interest are the changing of the name United Colonies to United States that occurred on September 9, 1776, and the adoption of the Articles of Confederation, which formally made the colonies a single nation. This occurred on November 15, 1777. Then

---

1. *Transcript from the Journals Of The Continental Congress*, 1774–1789. Vol. V, as quoted by Ronald W. Howland, *A Chronology of American Charts* (Poz Publications, 1998), 201. This book is far and away the best piece of research on the issue of the Declaration of Independence, and is certainly one of the best sources for charts on United States history in general. I say this even though I disagree with his conclusions about the time of the chart.

there is the little matter of whether we were really independent before the British surrendered at Yorktown, and so on it goes.

There seems to have been a general awareness even at the time that the events of July 1776 marked the end one of state of affairs and the beginning of another, and that the new entity evolved continuously into the United States of America. And there is the fact that Americans have always celebrated July 4 as Independence Day. This tends to eliminate July 2 as the day in question even though at the time John Adams, in a letter that he wrote to his wife, Abigail Adams, wrote that he thought the July 2 was the day that would be celebrated.

This leaves us with the question of what time of day on July 4. And this has long been a subject of conflict. But some progress has been made. Thanks to Howland's book[2] we now know for certain that Congress had not adopted the declaration as of 9:00 A.M. on July 4, 1776. This eliminates at a stroke a popular but extremely unlikely chart for somewhere around 2:17 A.M. on July 4. The *Transcript from the Journals Of The Continental Congress* clearly shows that the debate on the Declaration was the second item listed in the minutes. So we are left with some time on July 4, 1776, between the late morning and dinner time.[3]

Without going further into the merits of the various charts, one group of charts stands out in light of the events of September 11, 2001. That is a group of charts for a bit

---

2. See previous note.

after 5:00 P.M. For the purposes of this article, I am going to use 5:10 P.M. cast for Philadelphia. What makes this time so interesting is that, over the last year or so, a number of astrologers have been saying that, among all of the charts for the United States, if something spectacular and difficult should happen to the U.S. between early August 2001 and November 2001, then this particular chart would be strongly confirmed. Well, it has, and the 5:10 P.M. chart is strongly supported by what has happened.

---

3. Howland argues for the late morning based on his reading of the transcript plus a letter from Franklin and three other delegates that indicates that instructions were received for the defense of New Jersey and Pennsylvania in the morning. In the transcript there are two resolutions that pertain to this issue. One of them was made before the Declaration's adoption and the other was made afterward. The second resolution sounds very much like the instructions referred to in the letter from Franklin et al, which were given "in the morning." On this basis, the Declaration would have had to be adopted at around 11:00 A.M. Howland supports this time with a very sophisticated argument based on other charts that are important in the history of English-speaking nations. However, the first resolution made before the Declaration is rather similar in nature to the second and actually uses a peculiar phrase that is also found in the letter from Franklin et al. This phrase is "flying camp," a military term of the time. I think that Howland's historical evidence can be read either way, but that Franklin's letter could actually have been a reference to the time of first resolution combined with the contents of the second since both resolutions clearly refer to the same issue. This interpretation of the evidence allows the possibility of the later afternoon times for which there is considerable evidence. See Howland, 202–10.

Putting Events on the World Map

ROBERT HAND

M odern planetary astronomy allows astronomers to describe with accuracy when astronomical phenomena are going to occur. This gives modern astrologers an enormous advantage over the ancient astrologers who relied on the use of inaccurate planetary tables to calculate their charts. Once we know the astronomical phenomena, and when they are going to happen, we assume, because history bears this out, that the corresponding events will happen on the Earth as well.

Where Will an Event Happen?

Planetary combinations occur in the heavens and not on Earth. For example, the old-time astrologers would forecast the weather and would say that when the Sun was with Mars (what astrologers call a conjunction), the weather would be hot and dry. But where would it be hot and dry? It could not be true that the entire planet was hot and dry at once. Some places are never hot or dry. So, determining where would the Sun/Mars combination be most effective was a significant problem.

Early astrologers, such as Claudius Ptolemy (second century A.D.), related celestial events to places on the Earth by assigning certain signs of the zodiac to specific places. For example, Aries was said to rule the area around Palestine. Leo was said to rule the area around Italy, and so forth. Individual cities were also assigned connections with the signs of the zodiac, and this was done according to various criteria that varied from city to city. The idea was simple: If an astrological combination occurred involving a certain sign of the zodiac, then every region and every city connected to that sign was affected by that combination. Medieval almanac makers relied heavily on this system to make their predictions for the various parts of Europe.

However, astrologers discovered several problems with this traditional approach. The two biggest ones are these:

- The process of assigning regions and cities to the signs seems arbitrary and unsystematic; and
- The original system leaves out most of eastern Asia, southern Africa, and all of the Western Hemisphere. In other words, the system does not apply to any of the world that was unknown to the peoples living around the Mediterranean at about A.D.100.

Therefore, it became obvious to astrologers that a new approach to locating astrological effects upon the Earth was

vital if we going to be able to do anything of value in analyzing and forecasting events.

The solution to the problem was found in the twentieth
century. It is referred to generically as Astro Mapping, although it is most well known under the trademarked name
Astro*Carto*Graphy, which was created by the late Jim
Lewis. Astro Maps are maps that represent a specific time
during a planet's orbit. Lines on the map indicate where the
planets appear to rise, culminate (reach highest point, as
seen from Earth), set, and anti-culminate (reach lowest
point, as seen from Earth). These four points are known as
the *Angles* on a chart. See Figure 6 on page 244. The birth
chart for an event is examined first, and those planets located near the angles in the chart are considered strongest
and are given more importance by astrologers looking for
locations with high potential for events to occur.

The Angles: Ascendant, I.C., Descendant, Midheaven

At any given moment, some point in the zodiac is rising in
the east. We say the Sun is dawning, and astrologers call this
point the *Ascendant*, or rising sign. Likewise, at the same
time some point in the zodiac is setting in the west. This
point if referred to as the *Descendant*, and it represents the
western horizon point. The Sun is at its highest (culminating) and southernmost[1] point of the day when it is halfway
in time between its rising and setting time. This corresponds

---

1. Southernmost in the Northern Hemisphere, that is. In the Southern
   Hemisphere, that same highest elevation is the *northernmost* point of
   the Sun in the day.

to noon, more or less.[2] The point halfway between rising and setting is called the Midheaven, or in Latin *Medium Coeli*,[3] or by the abbreviation M.C. Halfway between sunset and sunrise the Sun hits a point lowest (anti-culminating) beneath the horizon and northernmost,[4] which corresponds to midnight.[5] The point of the zodiac that is halfway between setting and rising is called the only by the Latin *Imum Coeli*,[6] or by the abbreviation I.C.

Because astrologers have long known about the relationship between the planets and the angles, they have always paid the most attention to planets that are near these angles in a chart. So when charts were cast for New Moons, Full Moons, or eclipses of the Sun or Moon, it has always been considered necessary to take note of places on Earth where the planets are in relation to the angles. The idea is to be able to find where those places on Earth may be so that we can find out where each planet is most powerful at such

---

2. The reason for "more or less" is that our clocks keep a kind of "averaged out" time which is also set for some longitude on Earth near to our own but not precisely our own, except for those who live exactly on what are called "Standard Time Meridians." Our Eastern Time is set for a meridian of longitude 75 degrees west, Central Time for 90 degrees west, Mountain Time for 105 degrees west, and Pacific Time for 120 degrees west and so on. On top of that, for more than half of the year our clocks are set forward an hour with "Daylight Saving Time."

3. Which means exactly "midheaven."

4. Of course, again, in the Southern Hemisphere, the midnight Sun is at the *southernmost* point when lowest below the horizon.

5. Again, this is also "more or less" because of the averaged time and time zone issues just mentioned.

6. Which means "lowest point of heaven."

a time. For if we can, according to astrology we ought to be able to tell which parts of the world are going to be affected most strongly at a particular time, and by which planet.

Summer of 2001

The September 11 attacks came during the last days of summer with the Sun in the sign Virgo. However, the summer season began with the entry of the Sun into the sign Cancer. Therefore, to analyze the summer season as a whole, we would erect a chart for the exact moment that the Sun entered Cancer, and then look for the patterns that might lie behind the attacks. See Figure 7 on page 245. We will not look at the whole chart here, but only at the planet Neptune—a planet that is said to be connected with hidden and invisible matters, and, when its negative side shows up, with treacherous acts that are intended to cause weakening.

As we have said, at any time each planet is rising, culminating, setting, or anti-culminating as we see it from Earth. What actually happens is that all of the points where a planet rises and sets lie on a circle[7] that goes around the Earth. Figure 8 on page 246 shows the map of the Earth at the time of the Sun's entry into Cancer, with circles representing the places where Neptune was rising, setting, culminating, or anti-culminating.

We can see the circle representing Neptune on the MC (Midheaven) going down the Earth from north to south

---

7. This narrow band, or circle, is known as the ecliptic, which is the plane of the Sun's apparent orbit around the Earth. All the planets orbit within this band, which extends about 23.5 degrees north and south of the plane of the Earth/Sun orbital path.

cutting through the East Coast of the United States in the northeast. Over on the left side of the map, a white line shows where Neptune is rising. The problem with this globe type map is that we cannot see the places where Neptune is on the I.C., and where Neptune is setting respectively, because they are on the other side of the globe. So we want to use a standard type map that shows the entire world at once. See Figure 9 on page 247.

The vertical line on the left that extends through east Asia connects all those places where Neptune is on the I.C. The curving line on the left side of the map connects all those places where Neptune is rising. The vertical line cutting down through eastern North America connects all those places where Neptune is on the M.C., and the line curving through Europe and Africa connects all those places where Neptune is setting. The fact that rising and setting lines are curved and the M.C. and I.C. lines are straight is caused by the math used to turn the world from a sphere into a flat rectangle. As we saw from the globe map in Figure 8, both the rising and setting lines and the M.C./I.C. lines are really circles going around the world.

With the aid of Astro Mapping we can see all of the places on Earth that were strongly affected by Neptune at the time of the Sun's entry into the sign Cancer. It is the nature of these charts, erected for the beginnings of seasons, that they show indications for the following ninety days (roughly) until the next season begins. Even though the Sun, Moon, and planets (including Earth) continue in their orbits, the effects—as determined by the birth chart—will remain constant. Just as our genetic code is encoded at conception, the planetary imprint is fixed at the moment of a seasonal ingress, New Moon, or birth of any kind. The imprint will only be replaced when the Sun makes its ingress into the sign of the subsequent season, or another New Moon is born, for example.

Now that we have the idea of what Astro Mapping is we can look at a map of the world which shows us not only the planet Neptune but all of the other planets as well. See Figure 10 on page 248.

This map probably seems confusing because we have so many lines. One could say that with so many lines, no point on Earth is very far from being on one line or another. This is true, but we have to keep some things in mind. First, each part of the world is only affected by the planets whose lines pass through it, and in accord with the nature of that planet. The lines of each planet have different effects. Second, because this map of the entire world is drawn in a rather small format, it is easy to overlook the fact that places on Earth have to be rather close to a line to be strongly affected by the planet. The closer to the line, the more pronounced the effects, but some effects can be felt as far as 700 miles away.[8]

Even at this small scale we can see some large-scale patterns. Notice that the vertical M.C. and I.C. lines are strongly clustered over the West and East Coasts of the United States, and second over the Middle East. Note the especially strong group passing over Afghanistan. This suggests that these two

---

8. Jim Lewis & Ariel Guttman, *The Astro*Carto*Graphy Book of Maps* (Llewellyn, 1989).

areas will be centers of concern in the summer season of 2001. And before anyone asks whether any of us saw something coming like this, the answer is yes! Both myself and Jim Shawvan of San Diego wrote articles in the *Mountain Astrologer* magazine warning of warlike signs coming in 2001.[9]

Now let's look at a close-up of the United States. See Figure 11 on page 249. As we can see, several lines pass over the West coast. They strongly connect places through which they go to the energies of the chart as a whole. Here the Sun and Moon should be regarded as passing through the United States, not merely as passing through the western part of this country. Also notice that the Mars M.C. line passes off the West Coast. Putting this all together it suggests that the West Coast region is not strongly affected in any negative way by this chart, but that the United States as a whole is strongly affected.

But look at the East Coast! There we see the Neptune M.C. line passing very close to New York and the Saturn Asc. line passing through southern Maine. When United Airlines Flight 175 left Logan Airport in Boston, it flew due west until it passed over the Hudson River. It then headed due south into the North Tower of the World Trade Center. In doing so it turned south just past the Neptune M.C. line and then paralleled it down to New York City.

---

9. See Jim Shawvan, "The Red Planet and the White House: Mars in the Presidency of George W. Bush," in *The Mountain Astrologer*, April/May 2001 and Robert Hand, "A Crisis of Power: Saturn and Pluto Face Off," in *The Mountain Astrologer*, Aug/Sept 2001.

And what is the case with southern Maine? At least two of the hijackers boarded planes in Portland, Maine, and flew to Logan Airport in Boston. At Logan they switched to the transcontinental flights that crashed into the World Trade Center. Neptune at its worst, as we said earlier, is sneaky, hidden, and covert. Saturn at its worst is considered by astrologers to be the "Greater Malefic," a planet that can symbolize great harm.[10]

What About the Middle East?

Remember that the places where the Sun and Moon lines fall are especially important. The Sun M.C. and Moon M.C. lines, in this chart, pass right through Afghanistan and Pakistan. See Figure 12 on page 250. Remember that the I.C. lines for these two points passed through the United States. The Jupiter M.C. line goes over the Afghanistan/ Iran border, and next to it is the Mercury M.C. line. One of the surprises has been that Iran, for reasons of its own, has been not entirely hostile to our efforts to rout bin Laden and the al Qaida organization out of Afghanistan. Although Iran has no interest in helping us, it is not interested in helping the Taliban rulers of Afghanistan either. (In October, Iran agreed to assist and rescue any U.S. military personnel trapped on the ground.) Next to these, moving west, are the Mars I.C.

---

10. However, in both cases these are the planets at their worst. In the astrology of individuals and even in mundane astrology, which is what we are looking at here, both planets have positive and constructive sides as well. The problem is that more often than not in mundane astrology, not so much in natal astrology, the worst side is what comes out.

and Pluto I.C. lines respectively. These also pass through Iran and Saudi Arabia. All is not entirely sweet with Iran. Mars is the planet of war or anger, and Pluto suggests very deep obsessions and, like Neptune, is often associated with covert actions. These lines passing through Saudi Arabia suggest that this friend may not be quite the friend it seems.

Then we have the Saturn M.C. line passing through Yemen, Saudi Arabia, and Iraq. It actually goes quite close to the place in Yemen where the U.S.S. *Cole* was attacked in October 2000. The Saturn M.C. line passing through Iraq with the Saturn Ascendant line in southern Maine may indicate a connection between the two places. Did Iraq have anything to do with this? These lines are far from conclusive, but are very suggestive.

Conclusion

Other articles in this book will show the Astro Mapping technique in action more completely. It is only when Astro Maps of several charts point in the same general direction that one can really begin to sort out the lines and see which parts of the world are really going to be most affected.

Recommended Reading

The Clash of Civilizations and the Remaking of World Order by Samuel P. Huntington (Touchstone Books: February 1998).

"Twin" Events

STEPHANIE CLEMENT

This book focuses on terrorism and the aftereffects of terrorism, but its immediate focus is on the two, or twin, attacks on two seats of power in the United States. The first attack, on the twin towers, hit at the heart of New York City's financial district. The second attack, on the Pentagon, struck at the heart of our military and political power base—Washington, D.C.

One of the most fascinating things for an astrologer to consider is why two entities, twins, for example, often lead such different lives. This has been, in fact, one of the arguments used to invalidate astrology. Skeptics will ask, "If astrology can define an individual or an event, then tell me why twins, who are born at nearly the same time, can lead such different lives?"

The answer is: A person has the free will to act on his or her thoughts and desires in a manner that is in alignment with individual core beliefs and values. While the same astrological influences appeared in everyone's lives on September 11, a great many things were different. In astrology, the exact time and location of birth is unique to an individual, like a fingerprint is unique. And, in the same way that we are not drawn to every person we meet, neither are we drawn to respond to other influences in the same way as everyone else. We respond according to those characteristics (astrological, as well as acquired) that distinguish one person from another. And, even within the limitations of genetics and environment, we have free will.

Not everyone has secretly plotted during the past months, or years, to kill people and destroy property. Instead, they gathered ripe fruit, tended to household business and gardens, worked on projects, and accomplished critical thinking and problem-solving tasks. Millions of Americans were engaged in the various facets of these creative processes at the same time as a few terrorists were dedicated to and engaged in their destructive activities.

So what do these terrorist acts have to do with the astrology of twins? In my research on twins[1] I found that there is often a set of events that happen to the first-born twin and then to the second. There is a second set of events that happen to the second twin and then to the first. Then there are events that happen to one twin and never occur in the life of the second twin.

Here is an example: After one twin fell and injured her head severely, the mother worried that the second twin would have a similar accident. I was able to reassure her

---

1. Stephanie J. Clement, Ph.D., conducted an extensive study of birth twins, and she draws her conclusions from the more than 400 charts that she analyzed.

that the second twin was safe. The reason: The energy reflected in the chart of the injured twin would never appear
in the other chart—the astrological influence was past before the second twin was born.

Given the remarkably short time between most twin
births, this was surprising. However, the same effect occurred between the four plane crashes on September 11,
2001. Nothing could have prevented the hijackings, given
the current state of airport security. What did change dramatically were the results. The World Trade Center towers
were completely destroyed, but thousands of people escaped from the South Tower before it was hit and eventually collapsed.

The plane that struck the Pentagon and the plane that
crashed in Pennsylvania both are believed to have missed
the obvious primary targets of the White House and the
Capitol. The effective time had passed. How do astrologers
know this? Astrologers use the time of take-off of a plane to
assess the events of airplane flights—the take-off time is
the "birth" of that flight. The times of the four take-offs on
September 11 were within twelve minutes of each other.

Throughout this book you will read about events based
on the times of the crashes. This is because the crashes
themselves are major events, and each event has its own
"birth" chart. By analogy, each partner in a marriage has a
unique birth chart, but a chart for the marriage time is
used to track the marriage itself. The outcomes of the four
flights are reflected in the take-off charts. In fact, because
the four flights were part of one terrorist plot, the first take-
off time will accurately reveal the events. The subsequent

take-off times are comparable to the birth times of second and subsequent infants in a multiple birth.

The charts for the two crashes at the World Trade Center, the first at 8:46 A.M. and the second at 9:03 A.M., fall well within the normal interval between twin births. (There is disagreement in the media about the exact times of these crashes. Astrologers are leaning toward the two times mentioned here, but the authors of this book have used different times in their writing. There is always a question about whose clock was most accurate as well.)

As you will notice when looking at the two crash charts on pages 240–41, several planets are in different sectors. Astrological charts are divided into twelve sectors, or houses. Each sector is like a room in a house, and is suited to different kinds of activities of the chart. The planets that move into different sectors are Mercury, Venus, Saturn, and Pluto. I'll explain more about this later, but first let's look at the placement of the Sun in these charts and what that means in the attacks.

What an Event Chart Is and How It Works

In event charts, the Sun and Moon play very prominent roles. The Sun shows what the event is really about, and the Moon shows the action. The chart is somewhat like a play. The Sun is the overall plot, or theme. (The theme of *Hamlet*, for example, is about avenging the death of one's father.) And the Moon is the action that results from emotions and feelings. (The action in *Hamlet* occurs as Hamlet plots and schemes to get the proof he needs, as he builds his courage to take revenge, and, finally, as he takes action.)

An event chart is a chart set for the time of the event. Your birth chart is one kind of event chart—the event is birth in that case. In the chart of any event, the Sun's sign and location in the chart give an astrologer clues as to what the event is really about. In your birth chart, for example, the Sun sign tells what your personality and character are like. The Moon tells how your life is likely to unfold. This is true of the other planets as well.

Secret Plans Carried Out by Secret Followers

In the charts for the attack on the twin towers, the Sun is in Virgo. The following are generalizations about the sign Virgo, and as with or any other sign, they should be considered just that. Virgo is the sign of the follower. A Sun-sign Virgo may be following paths indicated by other factors in the birth chart, as well as the dictates of his or her own heart. Even the terrorists are following their own hearts when they devote themselves to their leaders.

Virgos are often willing to remain in the background, and that is especially true when the Virgo Sun is in the twelfth house. The twelfth house, for example, is suited to private, even secret activities. In the crash chart, the Virgo Sun may indicate that the planning was done by someone second in command to a more dynamic leader. This fact is borne out by an article filed by Joyce M. Davis of the Washington Bureau, which appeared in newspapers on October 15, 2001. Davis writes that Dr. Ayman al-Zawahiri, who was born in Egypt in 1951, is considered to be "the strategic genius who leveraged [Osama] bin Laden's largess into a well-organized terrorist campaign." Zawahiri is considered to be far more dangerous than bin Laden. He's the mastermind behind the concept of terrorist cells, and is very persuasive in recruiting people to do his work.[2]

We've learned from other news reports about the degree of training and planning that was necessary to succeed in the hijackers' plan to commandeer four or more planes and fly them to their targets. Evidence collected from the terrorists' homes and cars indicate that they researched airlines, flight paths, take-off times, and multiple other factors in planning these attacks. The terrorists dedicated their lives to carrying out their mission by becoming trained pilots, determining how to carry out their individual roles, and accepting suicide as a part of their actions. Their extreme attention to the details of the attack is consistent with what we know about Virgo. Virgos are inclined toward idealism; they are sometimes aloof or hesitant to participate fully in life; and they tolerate solitude well. It is important to keep in mind, however, that these activities represent only some facets of Virgo; there are many other Virgo qualities one can develop. The terrorists identified with what some would call the dark side.

There is some question among astrologers whether the Pentagon was a primary target.[3] There is no question, though, that the World Trade Center towers were the terrorists target. The Virgo Sun is in the sector of the chart com-

---

2. *St. Paul Pioneer Press*, October 15, 2001. The article is also available on-line at www.pioneerplanet.com/news.

3. See Kris Brandt Riske, "The Targets," in this book for a more complete discussion of the possible targets in these attacks.

monly identified with secrets, private activities, ambushes, plots, self-destruction, suicide, and treachery, in general. Traditionally, astrologers identify this area with secret or hidden enemies. It also has to do with the unconscious mind, the most hidden part of our psyches. The chart for the first crash reflects an action begun and carried out in secret by hidden enemies. The attacks were plotted in secret, perhaps years before they actually occurred.

Sign of the Twins

The Moon was in Gemini, sign of the twins, on September 11. It is often true that the events that occur while the Moon travels through the sign of Gemini involve two kinds of communication, or two kinds of action.

The Moon in Gemini indicates an intellectual quality. Emotions fluctuate—almost like they are blowing in a breeze. There is a restless quality, like a child who has just started to school and hasn't learned how to sit still. The Gemini Moon is more concerned with events and places outside the home.

The Moon on September 11 was waning (in the third quarter) as it was approaching the New Moon that would occur on September 17. This phase of the Moon reflects a crisis in consciousness. Something pushes us, after the event, to germinate new attitudes and to revise the way we have been acting.[4] The changes will be based upon thoughtful consideration of all the information available. (Note that

---

4. See Robert Hand, "Where Do We Go From Here?", in this book for a
   more detailed discussion of planetary cycles.

even while the United States attacked terrorist strongholds in Afghanistan, food and supplies were being airlifted to the Afghan people.)

In any event chart, the Moon reflects the action. In this case, the Moon was in Gemini in the ninth sector of the chart.[5] The Moon in this part of the chart shows us that the event involves travel. We had four planes and their crews and passengers traveling across the country. We also had terrorists who had traveled from distant countries to hijack the planes. Finally we had the planes traveling to crash into targets selected by the terrorists. All of these things were directly or indirectly involved with the crashes.

Mercury Delivers the Message

I've discussed the emotional nature of Gemini, but for me, the key to these twin events is the planet Mercury. In astrological terms, Mercury reflects the nature of intellect (how we think), language, and communications. Named after Hermes in Greek mythology, Mercury was the "messenger of the gods," and as such he carried communications back and forth between mortals living on Earth and the gods. Any link between distant places establishes communication, so the airline flights themselves were a kind of communication. Mercury is the fastest of the planets, orbiting

---

5. The Moon in the Ninth House, or sector, indicates public commodities and their traders, desks, drivers of vehicles, information and its dissemination, publishing, reporting, Saudi Arabia, stockbrokers, and trade or sales, among other things. People of many nations occupied the World Trade Center, and they engaged in all of the activities previously mentioned.

the Sun about three times a year. It accurately represents the nature of modern-day communication, which puts us in touch with reporters on the ground in Afghanistan in seconds.

In the hours following the attacks, Americans got two messages loud and clear. The first message was about safety. We understood that nothing is safe—not New York City, not Washington, D.C., not any location in the world, really. The second message was about power. We understood, for the first time, how powerful is the hatred of some individuals for Americans and our lifestyle, that they would go to great extremes to show us. We also learned the power of fear. Fear ground this bustling nation to a near standstill within mere hours.

Other messages and realizations have reached us in the weeks since the events. We are not willing to feel powerless for more than a few moments. Governments are working around the clock to find the best way to resolve the terrorist problem. Nations who haven't communicated with each other for decades are now expressing a willingness to sit down at the bargaining table and work out their differences. Individuals are making it their business to help others. The news media is spending large amounts of time informing the world about the issues behind terrorism.

Instead of being cowed into submission, the people of the United States and the world are saying, "Enough! We are thinking about our relationships, our alliances, and our lives differently. We want the world to be different." The United States government will take action. We can be proud that our leaders are giving careful consideration to our options before they act. They are enlisting the help of other nations. They are considering the innocent lives of millions of people in Afghanistan and other neighboring countries. They have focused on one target: terrorism. Our message to the terrorist organizations is clear: Don't think you can continue to act with impunity.

Venus and Social Consciousness

The role the planet Venus has in astrology is to bring love, harmony, beauty, and friendship into the world. What, you wonder, could any of those qualities have to do with the World Trade Center attacks? As with all things, there is an alternative to the love we associate with romance, marriage, family, or the love of material possessions. There is a dark love that is experienced as greed, lust for power, and obsession that can lead to destruction of life.

We know that the hijackers fervently believed in what they were doing. Their love and devotion to their cause, their lust for power over Americans and the world, carried them into a deep obsession that ended in death and terrible destruction. They were drawn, as if by magnets, to the power centers of the United States.

We know the terrorists acted out of devotion to their cause to remedy a situation that their leaders find unacceptable. We know they lived together as units, or cells, in order to help each other in the most basic ways. The people who helped each other out of the falling buildings, the firemen and police officers who forfeited their own lives to save others, and the thousands of rescue workers who worked tirelessly to find survivors—they were all responding to the situation with love, devotion, and friendship. Where the hijackers and terrorist organizations are drawn to the dark side of love and friendship, the victims and survivors of the attacks responded from the highest expression of love one individual can extend to another.

When Venus moved from the eleventh to the tenth sector, she moved into one of the most powerful parts of the astrological chart. She took up a position of public awareness and individual responsibility. Greater maturity is being called for on the part of all the people involved in dealing with the aftermath of tragedy. We are being required to consider the larger social issues that have resisted solution until now. The movement of Venus, into the light of public's awareness, suggests a path for us to follow through these events. The power we're being shown is that of cooperation on national and multinational levels. Our cooperation with each other will go far toward restoring financial stability, and renewing our sense of harmony and optimism.

The Saturn/Pluto Connection

Throughout this book, the authors make frequent mention of Saturn and Pluto and their relationship in the sky right now. They are in opposite parts of the heavens, very close to 180 degrees apart. Both planets move into different sectors of the charts for the World Trade Center crashes. This places a very high focus on the kinds of activities associated with these planets.

Saturn is a mythological character often associated with time. His activities are regulated, and astrologers associate this planet with serious activities, isolation, and a lack of adaptability. This means that at the time of this attack, there was less potential for a quick response than we would have liked. It also means that terrorism is a serious activity, and that we must take these people seriously. We cannot isolate ourselves and expect everything to be all right.

Pluto, the god of the underworld in mythology, is often associated with invisible forces, or the hand of providence. We saw the force of the underworld when the planes came out of the sky and crashed into buildings. In sharp contrast, we saw providence at work when many thousands of people escaped the crumbling buildings. Actions associated with Pluto are sometimes ruthless, fanatical, and coercive. I can think of few words that describe the action of terrorists better.

Together, Saturn and Pluto reflect qualities of cruelty, a tendency toward violence, and fanatical adherence to one's principles. This is not a fun combination. Even in a typical person's chart, this combination can indicate the need for radical surgery, a hard-hearted attitude toward others, and self-denial. Terrorists embody the extremes of this, at best, difficult combination of energies.

At this point I want to make it clear that we all have Saturn and Pluto somewhere in our charts, but not all of us are cruel fanatics. Most of us learn to temper our destructive urges. We can have less than admirable thoughts, but we choose not to act on them. More positive traits associated with this pair include hard work, the ability to strive for a goal when others have long since given up, and to search deeply for scientific answers, to name a few.

Because Saturn and Pluto are currently in opposite parts of the sky, astrologers look for events and situations that are obvious. Awareness is the quality most closely associated with this opposition. We certainly became aware of the cruel minds behind these attacks as the news unfolded in the aftermath.

The suspected perpetrators come from a religious tradition that includes suppression, cruel treatment of women, and what we can only think of as cold-heartedness in the extreme. We have to remember that that same tradition has included beautiful architecture, intellectual accomplishments, and the mystical wisdom of Islam and Sufism. We also have to mark the profound heroism of the firefighters, police, and emergency personnel who leapt into action in a situation that was to be their last act in this lifetime. Nothing is one-sided, least of all a combination of planets on opposite sides of the heavens.

The Other Pair of Planes

The second pair of hijacked planes apparently was headed for Washington, D.C. One crashed into the Pentagon and the other crashed in Pennsylvania. The second pair of charts associated with these crashes is only slightly different from the World Trade Center charts, yet those differences reveal the very different outcomes.

Even though the times of the crashes are approximately twenty-seven minutes apart, none of the planets move into different sectors. In fact, only the planet Uranus moves to a new sector from the second World Trade Center crash chart.

This is because the planets remain in the same sector for about two hours.[6]

As time moved forward from the first crash at the World Trade Center, the stress reflected in the astrological charts lessened.[7] It is possible that the hijackers on the later planes had more time to think about what they were doing. The adrenaline rush was leveling off, and they were slightly less intent on their goals.

While several well-known astrologers forecast that September would be a difficult period, and one even forecast an terrorist attack between September 11 and 13,[8] no astrologers could have pinned down the targets. However, if the United States were to be a target, the World Trade Center, the White House, and the Pentagon are all likely targets, as they symbolize the financial, political, and military might of this country, and, by extension, of the entire free

---

6. There are twelve sectors, or houses, in the chart. Therefore the planets move through each sector in about two hours time.

7. In the first crash chart (8:46 A.M. EDT) there were four quindecile (165 degree) aspects, including one from Mars to the Midheaven, within two minutes of arc exactness. This aspect indicated the obsessive nature of the attacks—the perpetrators were completely obsessed with their goals. In the chart for the second crash, the Mars Midheaven aspect is replaced by a quindecile from Neptune to the Midheaven, and this is a past aspect—it has already occurred. In the Pentagon and Pennsylvania crashes, there is no quindecile to the Midheaven or the Ascendant, indicating there was a lessening of the obsessive energy

8. Lynne Palmer, in her annual publication *Astrological Almanac for 2001* (Star Bright Publishers, 2000), chose this date months in advance of the actual day.

world. The terrorists are now discovering that they have turned public sentiment, even in predominately Muslim nations, against them. Few are willing to condone this kind of action, or at least no one is willing to step up and say they were involved.

Conclusion

It is my opinion that nothing could have been done to prevent this attack, short of changing our way of transacting business each day. The combination of the secrecy and the ordinary make it very difficult to eliminate any possibility of terrorist acts. Having seen these events, however, future airline hijackings will be far more difficult to accomplish. The passengers will not be so willing to sit still while a few people try to take over. The airlines and governments of the world will take stronger measures to prevent hijackings. These measures won't eliminate terrorism, but they will make it harder to perpetrate, at least on airplanes.

Structure Clashes with Beliefs

ROBERT HAND

Every thirty years or so Saturn and Pluto align in a single degree of the zodiac. This is called a conjunction.
About fifteen to nineteen years after this conjunction the
two planets come to opposite degrees of the zodiac. This is
called an opposition. This is a difficult combination in that
it indicates shortages, hard times, and a need for greatly increased toughness on the part of all those who experience it.

In the twentieth century all of the Saturn/Pluto combinations, whether by conjunction, opposition, or square
(halfway between), have coincided with wars of varying
severity, economic downturns, and, since World War II, periods of peak instability in the Middle East. Between August
5, 2001, and May 26, 2002, three oppositions of Saturn and
Pluto will occur.[1] The first of these was on August 5, the

---

1. There are three oppositions because Saturn and Pluto appear, from
our perspective on Earth, to move together, separate, and then move
together three times before Saturn moves away from Pluto and pro-
ceeds ahead alone.

second on November 2, and the third will be on May 26, 2002.[2] The August 5 and November 2 oppositions are the most significant for us because the first opposition occurred in the exact degree of the Ascendant, or rising degree, on the birth chart for the United States.[3] This singles out the United States as being a nation that would experience the effects of the opposition very strongly. The second opposition is not very far away from the first. However, the May 2002 opposition is quite far away from the Ascendant of the United States chart. If the 5:10 P.M. chart is correct (and based on September 11 events, we think it is) then it suggests that the most difficult parts of the anti-terrorist war will be over after November. But, because Saturn continues to move over the Descendant of the chart, it will still not be easy for some time.

What the Ascendant Represents

The Ascendant of a nation's chart is said to describe events that happen to the people, not so much to the government. While the Pentagon, a government building, was hit on September 11, the greatest damage was inflicted on people

---

2. The first opposition was on August 5, 2001, with Pluto at 12 degrees and 38 minutes of Sagittarius and Saturn exactly opposite at 12 degrees and 38 minutes of Gemini. The second, on November 2, is at 13 degrees and 49 minutes of Sagittarius and Gemini respectively. The third, on May 26, 2002, will be at 16 degrees and 35 minutes of Sagittarius and Gemini.

3. July 4, 1776, at 5:10 P.M. in Philadelphia. For more information about the United States birth chart, see Robert Hand, "The United States Chart," in this book.

who had little to do with the federal government—the people in the World Trade Center in New York City and on the planes that were hijacked. In fact, it is believed that several planes were targeted to crash into buildings in Washington, D.C., including the White House and the Capitol (United Airlines Flight 93 from Newark and two other later planes from Newark). Flight 93 crashed in Pennsylvania, and the other two were ordered to land before anything could be done with them. As a result, most of the havoc was wrought on members of the general public.

Other Interesting Clues in the World Trade Center Chart

There is some dispute about the exact time that the first plane hit the World Trade Center, with times ranging from 8:45 to 8:46 to 8:48 A.M.[4] Fortunately, this is not enough time to make much of a difference in the Ascendant. (One minute represents approximately one-quarter of a degree out of 360 total degrees.) The chart for this time shows that the Ascendant of the World Trade Center chart is conjunct Mercury.[5] Saturn in the sign of Gemini was making a trine (120 degrees) to the Ascendant/Mercury conjunction. A trine is considered to be a very strong and usually benign angular relationship, which usually results in a balance being

---

4. The 8:46 A.M. time has been used to calculate the chart mentioned in this article.
5. Chart Ascendant is 14 degrees Libra 21 minutes, and Mercury is 14 degrees Libra 18 minutes.

reached between differing energies, with the result that actions are easier and not forced by circumstances.

Other astrological factors alter this typical assessment, however. The two planets, Uranus and Neptune, are moving together (transiting) through the sign of Aquarius. When two planets are in the same sign, the midpoint[6] between them is very important. On September 11, 2001, the midpoint between Uranus and Neptune was exactly 120 degrees from the Ascendant/Mercury conjunction on one side, and from Saturn on the other.[7] This makes an equilateral triangle in the zodiac that astrologers call a Grand Trine.

Where the simple trine (120 degrees between two planets) is considered benign, the grand trine is not. It is a very strange and difficult arrangement of planets. There are several astrological factors involved in this grand trine. Those factors are:

- Mercury signifies an announcement or message, and has to do with transportation;

- Saturn indicates restriction and separation, and it is traditionally said to relate to falling buildings or ruins;

- Uranus indicates sudden or surprising events; and

---

6. The midpoint is determined by dividing the exact number of degrees between two planets or points by two.

7. Neptune was at 6 degrees and 21 minutes of Aquarius, and Uranus was at 21 degrees and 50 minutes of Aquarius. The halfway-point, or midpoint, was 14 degrees and 6 minutes of Aquarius.

- Neptune indicates weakness, hidden matters, and things that are not out in the open.

The entire combination could be read as something like this: A sudden event occurs, coming out of something secret having to do with restrictions, or possibly with falling buildings, and also involving transportation. Saturn in Gemini, and Gemini is strongly associated with Mercury, the planet rising across the Ascendant. So transportation is involved with a sudden manifestation of something secret. These combinations can be read in many ways but they all pertain very well to the events of September 11.

How does this relate to the chart of July 4, 1776? At 5:10 P.M. on that date, Saturn was at the exact degree that Mercury occupies in the chart of the first plane crash at the World Trade Center; meaning that it is tied in with our grand trine. Saturn in the 5:10 P.M. United States chart is close to the highest zodiac point in the sky, and, therefore, pertains to the government and its responsibilities. Saturn has a strong connection with money and economics. Here we can see the rather difficult economic effect that this is all having on our country.

Whatever may happen between now and the end of this struggle, it is evident that September 11, 2001, is a clear boundary line in the history of the late twentieth and early twenty-first centuries. Some have even called it the real end of the twentieth century.

What will be the long-range effect of all of this on our country? That is the subject of other articles in this book, such as "The New Investment Climate" on page 149.

All Eyes on Osama bin Laden

JONATHAN KEYES

In August 1996, Osama bin Laden sent out a proclamation of jihad (holy war or struggle) from Afghanistan. In his declaration, he wrote, "Message from Osama bin Laden to his Muslim brothers in the whole world and especially in the Arabian Peninsula: Declaration of jihad against the Americans occupying the land of the two holy mosques. Expel the heretics from the Arabian Peninsula."[1]

On February 23, 1998, *Al Quds*, an Arabic newspaper, published a proclamation by bin Laden and numerous other militant Islamic factions in Egypt, Pakistan, and Bangladesh. In their "Declaration of the World Islamic Front for Jihad against the Jews and the Crusaders," they stated that Muslims should kill American soldiers and civilians anywhere in the world.

---

1. "FBI Websites Document Evidence Against bin Laden," available online at http://usinfo.state.gov

In this second piece, that was published in full, bin Laden outlines the exact reasons why he is issuing this declaration of war:

"Since God laid down the Arabian Peninsula, created its desert, and summoned its seas, no calamity has befallen it like these Crusader hosts that spread in it like locusts, crowding its soil, eating its fruits and destroying its verdure; and this at a time when the nations contend against the Muslims like diners jostling around a bowl of food."

The proclamation continues after this poetic beginning to state the underlying reasons behind the declaration of war:

"First, for more than seven years, the United States has been occupying the lands of Islam in the holiest of its territories, Arabia, plundering its riches, overwhelming its rulers, humiliating its people, threatening its neighbors, and using its bases in the peninsula as a spearhead to fight against the neighboring Islamic people;

Second, despite the immense destruction inflicted on the Iraqi people at the hands of the Crusader-Jewish alliance, and in spite of the appalling number of dead, exceeding a million, the Americans nevertheless, in spite of all this, are trying once more to repeat this dreadful slaughter. It seems that the long blockade following a fierce war, the dismemberment and the destruction are not enough for them. So they come again today to destroy what remains of the people and to humiliate their Muslim neighbors;

Third, while the purposes of the Americans in those wars are religious and economic, they also serve the petty state of the Jews, to divert attention from their occupation of Jerusalem and their killings of Muslims therein. There is no better proof of all this than their eagerness to destroy Iraq, the strongest of the neighboring Arab states, and their attempt to dismember all the states of the region."[2]

It is from this fiery proclamation that bin Laden, the proclaimed head of the al Qaida organization, that we gain some of the answers for why he wages a holy war against the United States.

Osama bin Laden

Bin Laden is the youngest of twenty sons born to an immensely wealthy Saudi Arabian oil baron. Born into luxury, bin Laden became radicalized after he experienced three main events in his life: the United States–brokered peace accords between Egypt and Israel, the overthrow of the shah of Iran in an Islamic revolution, and the Soviet invasion of Afghanistan.[3]

After the Soviet invasion in 1979, bin Laden traveled throughout the Persian Gulf states to raise money to support a jihad against the Soviets. As he traveled through

---

2. "Text of Fatwah Urging Jihad Against American, *Al Quds al Arabi*, February 23, 1998; available online at www.ict.org.il, and link to articles.

3. Bernard Lewis, "Muslim Militants Reveal Different View of the World," *Oregonian: Foreign Affairs*, September 16, 2001, A14.

Afghanistan, bin Laden became enraptured with a group of militant Islamic fundamentalists from Egypt known as the Egyptian Islamic Jihad. This is the same group who helped to assassinate Egyptian president Anwar Sadat in 1981. In the 1980s, the United States and the CIA helped finance and train the rebels living in Afghanistan who were seeking to overthrow the Soviet regime. Bin Laden was one of the principal associates and allies with the United States during this time.

By 1986, bin Laden had established dozens of training camps in Afghanistan to fight the Soviets. It was in this year that bin Laden also established the al Qaida organization, the loose confederation of terrorist organizations that hoped to bring about a fundamentalist Islamic rebirth.[4]

Finally, in 1989, the Soviets admitted complete defeat. Though the Afghan people were euphoric that the Soviets had left, after United States aid dwindled, Afghanistan was left in ruins with many of its people dying of malnutrition, lack of adequate water supplies, and poor hygiene. Bin Laden believed that the Afghans were simply used as a tool by the United States to win its cold war with the Soviets, and he began to turn his anger towards Americans.

In 1991, the conflict between Iraq and the United States turned into the Gulf War. Many troops were stationed in Saudi Arabia, bin Laden's homeland. This further enraged him and after Iraq was defeated, bin Laden and al Qaida became galvanized to aim their attacks on the United States.

---

4. Judith Miller, "Terror's Money Now Jihad's Mastermind," *New York Times* News Service, September 16, 2001.

Terrorists planted bombs in the World Trade Center in 1993, hoping to destroy its foundations and topple the building. The plot failed, and the suspected terrorists were tied to bin Laden's organization. After the attempted bombing, followers of bin Laden bombed two outposts in Saudi Arabia, killing twenty-four U.S. soldiers. Then bin Laden targeted two embassies in Kenya and Tanzania, killing hundreds. And most recently, in October 2000, the navy vessel U.S.S. *Cole*, stationed in Yemen, was attacked by al Qaida suicide bombers, killing seventeen U.S. soldiers.

Afghanistan: A Country Ravaged by War

In order to better understand the reasons for bin Laden's enmity of the United States, its important to visit the history of the country where he resides, Afghanistan. In the landlocked country of Afghanistan, one in three children is an orphan, hunger is widespread, and only 12 percent of the nation have access to uncontaminated water. The people maintain themselves through raising livestock and farming. The past twenty years (since the Soviet invasion) have been times of tremendous turmoil and bloodshed. But conflict is not new to these people. They are enormously independent and fight fiercely to protect their country from foreign invaders.

The Great Game

Looking back into history, Afghanistan has always held a strategic location as a border country between Europe in the west and Asia in the east. It is the one nation that protected Pakistan and India from incursion by the Soviets in the Cold War. In the 1800s, both Britain and Russia vied for control of this vast mountainous region in what was known as the "Great Game." The British invaded Afghanistan in 1839 but withdrew four years later when they were unable to wrest control of this land. In 1878, Britain invaded again but then acceded to Abdur Rahman Khan after they were unable to maintain authority. Britain maintained troops there until 1919, when Rahman's grandson led an attack on British troops and took complete control of the country from foreign hands.

Afghanistan declared its independence in 1919, and developed a constitution in 1923. Throughout the subsequent decades, Afghanistan worried about a Soviet invasion and maintained good relations with non-communist countries. The Afghans flirted with a democracy in the 1960s, after years of royal rule, but it failed to develop. In 1978, leaders sympathetic to Communism and the Soviet Union took over Afghanistan but the tenets of this new regime clashed with the fundamentals of Islam and a rebel enclave known as the Mujahadeen revolted against this new government. To quell the rebellion and gain control of Afghanistan, the Soviets invaded in 1979.

This began a new stage in the history of Afghanistan. Soviet soldiers had many of the same difficulties the British had with defeating Afghan rebels. The terrain was harsh, supply lines were difficult and the natives knew the country well, were tough fighters, and used guerrilla tactics to fight off the invaders. The Soviets became bogged down in a war that resembled the United States' action in the Vietnam War. It was a war that was impossible to win and the Soviet troops became bogged down and demoralized.

End of the Cold War

In a larger framework, Afghanistan symbolized the end of the Cold War, as the former Soviet Union became financially unable to support an ongoing war. The Soviets retreated from Afghanistan and admitted defeat by 1989. The Soviet Union dissolved in 1991 and the old Communist party was overthrown.

With foreign governments' military and financial aid gone by the start of the 1990s, Afghanistan was left to fend for itself. The Muhajadeen were able to successfully overthrow the government by 1992 and set up their own regime but the fighting between various rebel factions continued.[5] By 1996, a group known as the Taliban was able to effectively gain control of 90 percent of the country. The Taliban's strict interpretation of the Koran virtually imprisoned women, who were required to wear the *burqa* (traditional women's dress), were no longer allowed to go to school, drive cars, sing, laugh out loud, work, or even speak to men who were not members of their family. Punishment is harsh for criminals and religious differences are not tolerated.

In the year 2000, the Taliban began to blow up ancient Buddhist statues. Nations from throughout the world, including Pakistan and India, decried the destruction of the statues and tried to dissuade the Taliban from their efforts, but to no avail. Most recently, the Taliban has jailed eight

---

5. Molly Moore, "Bin Laden Cash, Recruits Built up Taliban," *Los Angeles Times-Washington Post Service*, September 16, 2001. Molly Moore and Kamran Khan, "Afghanistan Campaign a Daunting Task," *Los Angeles Times-Washington Post Service*, September 18, 2001, and online at www.afghan-web.com/history.

foreign workers for preaching Christianity. They were put in prison and were awaiting trial when the recent attacks unfolded in the United States.

The Taliban and bin Laden have an intricately tied relationship. Bin Laden has supplied much of the training and financial backing to support the Taliban's regime. In turn, the Taliban has sheltered and supported bin Laden while he lives in the mountainous region of Afghanistan.

Astrological Perspectives

To understand the recent turn events from an astrological perspective, its important to look at several key factors, the most important one being the strong connection between Uranus and Neptune from 1989 to 1997.[6] (This conjunction has not been seen since the 1820s.) This time signified the dramatic transformation of bin Laden's aims from ridding Afghanistan of Soviet domination toward war against the United States. The Uranus/Neptune conjunction also triggered the collapse of the Soviet Union as well as the Gulf War. Astrologically, Uranus is associated with sudden change and Neptune is associated with spirituality, mass consciousness, and oil. Along with the Soviet Union's collapse and their retreat from Afghanistan, the United States went to war with Iraq over issues of oil. This is a very crucial aspect of the situation that is going on today. Though there was a desire to save Kuwait from Iraqi domination,

---

6. An 8 degree orb conjunction between Uranus and Neptune began on January 9, 1989, in Capricorn. The final separating conjunction occurred on December 21, 1997.

there was also a more compelling need for the United States to protect its oil interests in the region. Since the Arabian countries own much of the oil in the world, it was deemed essential in terms of foreign policy to secure the countries that supplied us with oil.

This Uranus/Neptune conjunction continues to be a part of the equation today. Much of the struggle that the United States has involved itself in the Middle East has to do with ensuring a steady supply of oil to the West. The Unites States supports regimes in Saudi Arabia, Egypt, and Kuwait that are not democratic but still act as friendly allies to this nation. The revolutions in Soviet bloc countries and the end of the Cold War that took place from 1989 to 1991 created a change in the consciousness of fanatical Muslims towards a deeper hatred for the United States. Instead of choosing a path of engagement with the Arab world, we have chosen a path of deeper isolationism in the past ten years. Our continued support of Israel has also encouraged Arabic anger to foment. This is not just anger from fundamentalists but anger from much of the Muslim world who perceive the United States as arrogant and only concerned with its own policy objectives.

With astrological conditions,[7] much of this deep-set anger is beginning to manifest against United States interests. We, as Americans, have a choice, however, in how we will respond towards that anger. Will we move toward an increasing escalation of violence and retribution, or will we

---

7. Saturn in Gemini opposing Pluto in Sagittarius.

instead move toward changing the structure of our foreign policy, toward understanding the root cause of suffering and enmity in the Middle East. Through dialogue with Muslim-dominated countries and exploration of religious issues as well as how cultural differences separate our worlds, there is a chance for a transformation of consciousness in the American people and its government.[8]

Astrology is a study of the movements of the planets and their interpretation as a symbolic language. The manifestation of these symbols and how they express themselves has partly to do with our choice. If we choose to see this as a time to exact revenge for an awful and devastating blow to the United States we may ensure a deeper level of pain and confusion that may return to us in an even more damaging way. If on the other hand we see this as a time for searching for the root causes of this suffering and hatred, we can ensure a better level of safety for United States citizens than simply with unmitigated war. This is a transformative time, a time to search deep into our collective psyche and find a place for understanding as well as justice, for patience and compassion as well as anger. The symbolic language of the planets can point us in many different directions. How we choose to proceed is up to us.

---

8. Again, this analysis is based on Saturn in Gemini in the Seventh House of United States chart, having to do with the structure of our foreign policy and how we engage in dialogue, in opposition to Pluto in Sagittarius in the First House, having to do with transformation of American consciousness and how we direct our will.

The Targets:
Hit or Missed?

Kris Brandt Riske

Founded by rebellious British subjects in 1776, America has grown to prominence through her establishment of, and adherence to, a set of values that include: democracy, home ownership, family, freedom, religious and political acceptance, and an independence that is foreign to anyone not calling themselves an American. Americans have fought and died on foreign soil to protect our freedoms and the freedoms of others.

Symbols of Democracy

Terrorists, believed to be disciples of Osama bin Laden's organization, al Qaida, staged a attack on America on September 11, striking her symbols of capitalistic freedom, military might, and governmental democracy. There is no doubt that the World Trade Center towers were targets, but many doubt that the Pentagon was a primary target. Did they intend to strike the Capitol Building? Did they intend to crash into the White House? Did they plan to kill the government of the United States of America? Astrology does offer some answers to these questions, and to find them astrologers study the birth chart for the buildings in question.

What Were the Real Targets?

In the days following the attacks, there was much discussion in the government and in the news media about what was the *real* target of hijacked American Flight 77 that departed from Dulles International Airport. Although the exact flight path is unknown, because the planes' transponder had been turned off, Flight 77 apparently turned around over southern Ohio and retraced its route over Virginia.

The *Washington Post* reported that soon after losing contact with the plane, Dulles controllers spotted an unidentified aircraft speeding toward the restricted airspace that surrounds the White House. Federal aviation sources said Dulles controllers noticed the fast-moving craft east-southeast of Washington Reagan National Airport and called controllers there to report that an unauthorized plane was coming their way. Controllers had time to warn the White House that the jet was aimed directly at the presidential mansion and was traveling at a gut-wrenching speed.

But just as the plane seemed to be on a suicide mission in to the White House, the unidentified pilot executed a pivot so tight it reminded observers of a fighter jet. The plane cut 270 degrees to the right to approach the Pentagon from the southwest, whereupon Flight 77 fell below radar level, vanishing from controllers' screens.[1]

Was the White House the Target?

The White House was the target of another suicidal pilot in 1994, when Frank Eugene Corder stole a single-engine plane shortly before midnight on September 11 from an airport north of Baltimore. The next day, Corder flew the stolen plane low over the White House South Lawn, clipped a hedge, skidded across the green lawn that girds the South Portico and crashed into a wall two stories below the presidential bedroom,[2] He died on impact. President and Mrs. Clinton were sleeping across the street at Blair House while workers repaired faulty ductwork in the White House.[3]

History tells us that the first cornerstone of the White House was laid October 13, 1792. Massive and imposing in one respect, the White House is also a building of grace and refinement. It serves as the official gathering place for social functions involving heads of state, elected officials, and others invited to dinners hosted by the president. Its chief resident is saddled with the responsibility for a nation, making the White House a place of work.[4]

---

1. *Washington Post*, September 12, 2001.
2. Michael Duffy, "The White House," *Time*, September 26, 1994.
3. The transiting planets in aspect to the White House horoscope were a near-miss on September 12, 1994. Had the suicidal pilot elected to fly the plane on September 11, the outcome might have been different.
4. The Libra Sun opposing Saturn in Aries combined with the Moon in Virgo speak to the dual functions of the White House, as well as its functionality, size, and beauty.

The White House is a building where decisions are weighed and made, where secret political battles are fought, and where intellect and diplomacy dominate. Changing power, like the changing of the guard, is the norm at the White House every four or eight years as presidents and their families move in and out.[5]

Timing for a strike on the White House was not in the terrorists' favor. But the astrological indicators signal it as a probable target, either of Flight 77 or United Flight 93, which crashed in Pennsylvania; or another unknown flight. Other astrological indicators suggest the plane made a last- minute change in course. The outcome might have been different had the attacks occurred later in the day.[6]

---

5. A Venus/Jupiter conjunction in Scorpio indicates secret negotiations, and the Sun and Mercury in Libra favor decision making and diplomacy. Mars in Sagittarius signifies foreign relations, and a Uranus/ Pluto opposition with a sextile/trine to the Sun is symbolic of the ongoing changes in administration and, thus, residents.

6. The White House birth chart (October 13, 1792) has a nearly exact Uranus/Pluto opposition, which was activated September 11, 2001, by transiting Venus and Uranus conjunct Pluto. Transiting Saturn was within nine minutes of progressed Venus, and Pluto was a little more than a degree from conjunction with natal Mars. The most telling factor of a potential disaster is progressed Mars forming a T-square with the natal Uranus/Pluto opposition (fifteen minutes from exact square to natal Pluto). The transiting Moon trine natal Neptune and sextile natal Saturn suggest the pilot's change of course, a missed target but a successful mission. At the time Flight 77 crashed into the Pentagon, the transiting Ascendant was two degrees past an exact conjunction with the White House Sun and a trine/sextile to the Uranus/Pluto opposition. Had it been later in the day, as the Moon was in the early degrees of Cancer, it would have activated transiting Mars, which was approaching a sesquisquare to progressed Uranus.

Was the Capitol Building a Target?

Again, we look at the chart for the date the building was started to find answers. Construction of the Capitol building began in 1793, but it was not fully completed until 1813 because of the need for additional wings to accommodate a growing Congress. William Thornton, a Scottish-trained physician living in the British West Indies, designed the building. He requested permission to submit a late entry to the design competition, which had produced seventeen plans that were deemed unsatisfactory. President George Washington laid the cornerstone on September 18, 1793, thus giving birth to the building.[7]

The Capitol building is a place of work, a place for the people's voice to be heard. Those working in the building are reminded of their responsibilities and the need to put service above ego.[8] The building best serves practical thinkers, those who focus on the nuts and bolts of things, without allowing emotion to enter the equation.[9] Nevertheless, the Capitol

---

7. The birth chart is used to identify an individual's talents, abilities, strengths, and weaknesses. It is erected for the date, time, and place the person is born. The branch of astrology that encompasses current events, weather, economics, and buildings also uses birth charts. In the case of a building, the start of construction, or the laying of a corner-stone, represents the building's birth. It reveals much about the actual building, the purpose for which it is used, the people who use it—in essence, everything that encompasses daily life.

8. In the chart for September 18, 1793, the Sun, which is in the sign Virgo (work and daily habits), Venus is conjunct Mars in Leo (prominence), and Saturn is in Taurus(practicality and responsibility).

9. The Pisces Moon opposes Mercury in Virgo. Both Virgo and Pisces govern service, in this case, service to country.

suggests the presence of power plays within its walls: senators and representatives jockey for position, trade favors, negotiate deals behind the scenes, and enact and repeal laws. Business at the Capitol is in a constant state of flux.[10]

The building itself is a monument to the American work ethic, representing freedom and justice for all. Renovations are almost a way of life at the Capitol; the building has been refurbished and, in previous years, was added on to accommodate the need for more office space. Today, the Capitol has a floor area of about 16.5 acres, including a museum of American art and history.

Was the Capitol building, seat of America's legislative branch and democracy's ultimate symbol of freedom, the real target of Flight 77? The potential was there from an astrological perspective, but the factors representing the deeply rooted essence, purpose, and foundation of the building were not affected on that day. Timing is often said to be everything, and that was true at the Capitol on September 11, 2001. Had the Capitol been built a few days, months, or years earlier or later, the outcome might have been different. The same would have been true if the time frame of the attack had been later in the day.

The Pentagon

Some speculated that, had the Pentagon been the real target, the pilot would have crashed the plane into the north

---

10. A T-square between Jupiter, Uranus, and Pluto, indicates power to change laws. The T-square is also symbolic of freedom and power with laws and justice as the intermediary to balance the two.

side of the building where high-level military and civilian personnel have their offices. Eyewitnesses said one of the planes' wings struck the ground, after which the plane spiraled into the Pentagon.

The massive five-sided structure was built just before the United States entered World War II. The groundbreaking ceremony took place on yet another September 11, this one in 1941. The building, the idea for which came from Brigadier General Brehon B. Sommervell in mid-July 1941, was built as a temporary solution to a growing War Department that occupied seventeen buildings in Washington, D.C. The first occupants moved into the Pentagon on April 29, 1942, and construction was completed January 15, 1943, at an approximate cost of $83 million.

The Pentagon's innovative design facilitates communication and traveling from one section of the building to another. Before the attack on it, which caused an estimated $1 billion in damages, the Pentagon had 17.5 miles of corridors. Interestingly, it takes only seven minutes to walk between any two points in the building because of its unique design.

Above all, the Pentagon is a building dedicated to work and service, to waging war on occasion, but always to maintaining peace. Serious business takes place there, as well as creative strategic planning. Peacemaking, though, is far more often the subject of discussion than is making war.[11] High principles, especially with regard to liberty and

---

11. Mars in Aries opposing Venus in Libra characterize the Pentagon's horoscope, that also features a Virgo Sun and Moon conjunct Saturn, and Saturn trine Neptune. Mercury in Libra centers thought and discussion on peacemaking.

justice are evident, and all possible effort is devoted to meeting and exceeding those ideals.[12]

Planetary configurations suggest the Pentagon might have been an alternate target that resulted from a last-minute change in plans. Had the pilot and the astrological indicators themselves been more accurately aligned, much of the building would have been destroyed, and many more lives lost. The attack was of course an unexpected one to the nation and Pentagon workers. It may have been the same for the hijacker-pilot.[13]

Recommended Reading

Capitol Building at www.cr.nps.gov/nr/travel/wash, National Register of Historic Places Travel Itinerary.

White House at www.pbs.org/wnet/whitehouse/timeline, Echoes from the White House.

Pentagon at www.defenselink.mil/pubs/pentagon, About the Pentagon.

---

12. Uranus in Gemini trine Mercury signal innovation, both in the building's design and in defense strategies. The Venus/Jupiter trine and Sun/Jupiter square reflect high principles.

13. Aspects involving Mercury and Uranus suggest a last-minute change as well as the unexpectedness of the attack. The transiting Sun was conjunct the natal Sun in a sextile to progressed Sun, that was activated by transiting Venus. The transiting Moon was trine progressed Mercury and square progressed Neptune. However, the Pentagon's horoscope does not reflect the same significant contact from the transiting Saturn/Pluto opposition that is seen in the White House horoscope.

Life Has Changed Dramatically

DAVID CROOK

Life has changed dramatically since September 11, 2001. Our collective angst, and a foreboding fear of what the future may bring, has certainly upset the status quo. Business as usual is not an option. But every crisis we confront, or are confronted by, is an opportunity for healing and transformation. This is difficult to understand, unless we are able to detach ourselves somewhat, and shift our worldview, in order to arrive at a sense of the bigger picture.

From an astrological perspective, we were aware that the current pairing of the planets Saturn and Pluto indicates stressful, challenging times. But as nature is ultimately neutral, it is up to us in to act out the highest possibilities of the times, based on a real understanding of the underlying dynamics. It is erroneous to think we are fated to be simply victims of planetary influence. This is a misunderstanding of the astrological paradigm, for we can shape the future to a great extent.

The astrology of world trends and every day events is called mundane astrology. This is actually the study of the cyclic nature of change. "The only constant is change. But if one understands the laws and principles that govern change, than one has a greater control of ones destiny."[1] We've said that astrology mirrors the meaning behind change; it can also indicate when these changes are likely to occur. This kind of information is invaluable if we wish to grasp a sense of our collective and affect social change.

One important astrological indicator involves Saturn and Pluto. The thirty-seven year cycle that informs many of the events that are occurring now began on November 8, 1982.[2] The profound potential of this particular combination of planets is only now becoming clear as we reach the halfway point in this cycle.[3] Energies and events are coming to a head at this halfway point. As Martin Luther King Jr. once said, "There is nothing more powerful than an idea whose time has come."

In 1982, the seed ideas and energies emerged, and they were sharply focused on Afghanistan.[4] Now that we have reached the peak of this cycle, we can see the potential un-

---

1. Richard Wilhelm, *I Ching* translation (Princeton University Press, 1967).

2. Saturn and Pluto were in the same degree at that time.

3. See Robert Hand, "Where Do We Go from Here?" in this book for a complete discussion of the effects of planetary cycles.

4. When the conjunction of Saturn and Pluto took place, on November 8, 1982, these planets were on the eastern horizon in Kabul, and Kandahar, Afghanistan.

folding in a dynamic fashion.[5] The natures of Saturn and Pluto are not intrinsically negative by any means. However, given our current level of consciousness in the world, it appears we must undergo a crisis period, in order to learn some necessary lessons. This process of upheaval, restructuring, and transformation will challenge many social and economic structures that are no longer viable.

Astrologically, Saturn represents the status quo and our natural drive for control and authority. The material world in which we live, with all its boundaries and limitations, is related to Saturn. We need laws and a certain amount of structure in order to live together in harmony. Sometimes the rules of society are imposed on us and we either bend, or rebel. Saturn also represents our resistance to change. Rigidity, and dogmatic attitudes that perpetuate a "business as usual" kind of thinking, are characteristic of Saturn. Again, the drive that Saturn represents is neither good nor bad, but is determined by its expression.

The planet Pluto, on the other hand, is symbolic of our need to wield power and influence. The inevitable processes of death, rebirth, healing, and transformation, are some of the dramatic themes linked with Pluto. Something must die so that something else can be born. But we tend to resist change in its many forms, and hence experience pain and suffering. Pluto signifies our need for periodic purging and cleansing of deep-seated emotions. The image of the snake

---

5. The first opposition of Saturn and Pluto occurred August 5, 2001. The second takes place November 2, 2001, and the third on May 26, 2002.

shedding its own skin, or a phoenix rising from the ashes, are useful metaphors for the process that Pluto represents. Healing often comes initially in the form of a crisis.

Saturn is currently moving through the sign of Gemini, while Pluto is transiting Sagittarius. Gemini is associated with the gathering and dissemination of information, while Sagittarius relates to ideas and ideologies. Some of the obvious correlations of Saturn and Pluto in these signs, with world events, was the recent closing of thousands of Internet cafes in China by the Communist government. The information flow and access to it has been curtailed by a controlling and repressive regime. In a similar move, several weeks before the September 11 attack on the World Trade Center, the ruling Taliban logged the whole nation of Afghanistan off the Internet. These are overt expressions of the current planetary potential, manifesting in a perverted manner, through the actions of those whom would dominate and repress freethinking.

The deep-seated racial, ideological, and religious conflicts that seem to be erupting all over the world reflect this same astrological combination. Followers of rigid belief systems are responsible for a great deal of the violence in the world today. There is a conspicuous lack of religious tolerance and acceptance at this point in time. The ongoing conflicts in Israel, Algeria, Ireland, Indonesia, Nigeria, and now Afghanistan, are only a few examples that immediately come to mind. But from an astrological perspective, a real opportunity for world healing and transformation is surely opening to us at this time. The planetary symbolism of

Pluto and Saturn reminds us that sometimes we need to breakdown in order to breakthrough.

Sagittarius is naturally associated with travel and the travel industry. With Pluto in this sign, a certain amount of renovation and restructuring of the airline industry, and other aspects of the travel business, could be foreseen. But the events that would trigger such a process, and the extent of its scope, probably could not have been predicted. As of this writing, in September 2001, the U.S. government has provided fifteen billion dollars in relief to keep the major airlines aloft, and now the major issue of increased safety needs at airports needs to be addressed in a comprehensive and uniform manner. The ongoing investigation last year involving Ford trucks and Firestone tires was the first sign of a potential shake-up in the travel and transportation business.

These examples are representative of a few events that reflect this process of breakdown and contraction that is informed by the current combination of Saturn and Pluto. Our collective loss of innocence, the result of the recent attacks on the United States, may have instilled a greater respect for the fragility of life, but has also given rise to a new level of fear and mistrust. The threat of loss is a key meaning of Saturn with Pluto, but so is the sheer determination, and persistence to overcome any and all difficulties. Life circumstances challenge us to be strong and unwavering in our resolve, despite our gnawing fears that we may not be up to the challenges before us. Paranoia has displaced faith and trust, in the hearts of many. This is a distorted manifestation of the current planetary trends. Nature is neutral.

We can each only live out the planetary trends at our own level of awareness.

Beginning with the birth chart for George W. Bush, we will explore some of the relevant dynamics at work in the current conflict with the Taliban-ruled Afghanistan, and attempt to get a sense at how the situation there may play out. I believe we may achieve at least a broad brushstroke picture, of the prospective landscape of world affairs, by examining a few of the important astrological charts, that provide a meaningful context for unfolding events.

One of the key features of George W. Bush's horoscope, or birth chart, is the planet Pluto rising at the Ascendant. This suggests a power-oriented individual who may be acting out some collective drive for control and domination.[6] The planet Uranus is strongly placed in his chart, indicating that Mr. Bush can be somewhat erratic at times, or willful and unorthodox in his behavior.

When astrologers first examined the inauguration chart for President Bush, they noted the stressful configurations that might easily be interpreted as signs of prospective conflicts or actual warlike conditions. The potential tension reflected in the chart is now taking shape, and will continue to do so for the next several years. But it's been noted, specifically in relation to the birth charts for American presidents, that a difficult chart may be exactly what is needed to deal with difficult situations. This type of thinking can be applied to both this inauguration chart, and Mr. Bush's natal map.

---

6. Uranus is the planet highest in the sky (this is called "elevated" by astrologers).

Mundane astrologers make use of charts drawn for each Solstice and Equinox, using the location of the capital city of a nation. These charts help us to understand how and where potential influences may unfold. These are referred to as solar, or cardinal ingress charts. The word ingress means "entering into," and the Sun enters a new sign at the beginning of each season: Aries in spring, Cancer in summer, Libra in fall, and Capricorn in winter.

The 2001 Fall Equinox, or Libra ingress chart, cast for Washington, D.C., shows Mars powerfully placed.[7] This suggests the government may tend to be aggressive in asserting its will, as Mars is assertive, even combative. The crucial opposition of Saturn and Pluto in the houses of international relations suggests a focus on foreign affairs, and the potential for conflicts with other nations.

One place in particular the Libra ingress seems especially potent is Israel, where we find Saturn, Pluto, and the Moon all prominently placed. This represents the potential for extreme events, and violent upheavals for through the end of 2001. (On October 5, 2001, after this article was written, a Russian airliner carrying seventy-six people including scores of Jewish holiday celebrants traveling from Tel Aviv to central Siberia, exploded and plunged into the Black Sea. It is now believed that a stray missile launched

---

7. Mars is close to the Midheaven in the Tenth House, an elevated position, as mentioned earlier in this article.

by the Ukrainian military was responsible for this tragic mishap, but that has yet to be confirmed.)[8]

December 1 signals a time when negotiations could proceed in earnest. Through mid-December, expect communications to take a number of different directions. New key players may emerge to establish publicly what the goals are for any negotiation.

In late December, if significant progress has not been made towards peace, there could be more demonstrations of strength in escalated fighting.

In late January 2002, the chart for the State of Israel is showing signs of increased stress, which could mark a volatile period for this country.[9] And the prospect for difficulties, is somewhat supported by tense aspects to Ariel Sharon's natal chart.[10] Although most eyes will likely be on Afghanistan, Israel remains one of the violent hotspots on the planet. It may be worth mentioning here, that the United States and Israel have strong astrological ties, and the support shown for Israel by the United States is a big reason that the Arab world hates this country.

The second opposition of Saturn and Pluto occurs on November 2, 2001, and could intensify the global tension

---

8. "Russia Blames the Ukraine for Crash," Associated Press, October 16, 2001, http://dailynews.yahoo.com

9. Progressed Mars squares Uranus, and transiting Uranus is still squaring the Sun. Both these aspects indicate haste and tension.

10. Ariel Sharon, born February 27, 1928, 7:49 A.M. EET, in Kafr Malal, 34E54, 32N11. The data source is Astrodatabank. A few of the closest contacts include solar arc Node conjunct Neptune, Solar arc Uranus conjunct the Node, and solar arc Mars conjunct the Ascendant, with transiting Mars conjunct the Ascendant on February 4, 2002.

level. Remember that Afghanistan is strongly connected with this current cycle of Saturn-Pluto, as these planets were near the eastern horizon in both Kandahar and Kabul, at the conjunction of November 8, 1982. So the potential energies and ideas seeded at that critical moment are linked with Afghanistan, in a very direct way. Events here will tend to mirror this unfolding cycle, as they are even now, at the climactic opposition phase of Saturn and Pluto.

At the December 30, 1999, conjunction of Pluto and Chiron, these two were conjunct the Ascendant in Washington, D.C., and closely at the Descendant (western horizon) in Kabul, Afghanistan. So we see from this that, both of these places are dynamically linked with the potential meaning of this planetary cycle, and will continue to respond as it unfolds in time. In fact, the national chart for Afghanistan has a challenging contact between Pluto and Chiron, while the inauguration map for President Bush, shows the Moon linked with both of these.

When we look at the world today, and the unnatural imbalances we have somehow brought about, it seems clear that a paradigm shift is in order if we wish to not only save ourselves, but aspire to a more conscious existence in harmony with the cosmos. Astrology grants us the perspective to understand the meanings of the times, and our unique place and purpose, in a much wider context.

Forecasting with Eclipses

DAVID CROOK

E clipses of the Sun and Moon are regularly occurring phenomena used in astrological forecasting. The places touched by the eclipse path itself are often those most directly involved with the energy it reflects,[1] but the eclipse chart itself, cast for a capital city, or seen in relation to a national chart, will provide indications of its relevance to that place. An eclipse casts a shadow, at least several weeks before it actually occurs, making exact timing of events difficult to predict, but generally, the effective time period of a solar eclipse is three to six months.

The solar eclipse of December 14, 2001, indicates issues around power, racial bias, hatred, and religious violence, which are now being brought into the light. Pluto represents the healing principle that forces the collective to experience

---

1. For information on eclipse paths, go to www.usno.navy.mil.

violent phases of self-healing in order to get well.[2] The path of this eclipse was largely in the Pacific Ocean, but it did pass through the center of Costa Rica and the southernmost part of Nicaragua. Things have been relatively quiet in Central American though this crisis, but we could see a blip on the political radar in December 2001 or January 2002. One interesting thing about Costa Rica is that President Rodriquez has suggested switching to a larger sugar crop for the Canadian market, as the coffee market has been weak recently. Canada has increased the sugar quota for Costa Rica, and may increase it again in the next few years.[3]

Although the actual path of the eclipse does not pass through Kabul, the chart does suggest a concern with international relations and probable difficulties in this arena. Jupiter in the chart indicates that the leaders of Afghanistan are likely dealing with neighbors and foreign affairs at this time, from an excessively, moralistic point of view. Financial and material resources will be a source of concern at this time as well.

A solar eclipse on June 10, 2002, indicates a period that will likely be disruptive to business as usual, and may tend to destabilize shaky situations even further. For Washington, D.C., we can expect a heavy dose of the energies of Saturn and Pluto—restrictions, our responses to problems; transformation of our vision of isolation versus world cooperation; and restraint in the use of military power.

---

2. This eclipse effects his Second and Eighth Houses, and contacts his Moon.
3. "Costa Rica Urges Shift to Sugar," is available online at http://dailynews.yahoo.com., and search "Costa Rica."

In relation to President Bush's inauguration chart,[4] this eclipse suggests more concerns with the economy and issues involving the citizenry. The Moon generally signifies a nation's common people, the domestic scene, and security. So the eclipse will primarily affect the area of resources, but secondarily, it may coincide with renewed fear of threats to our security here in the United States.

For Afghanistan, the issues focus on national identity and self-image. There is an urge to act out destructive motivations. For Saudi Arabia, the eclipse suggests a deep transformative process of social revolution. We can anticipate dramatic developments in Saudi Arabia up to October of 2004. There may be undermining of the ruling party and its leaders, as well as diminished power of resistance on the part of the Taliban there during 2002, and can also be interpreted as signifying extreme, emotional fanaticism.

The total solar eclipse of December 4, 2002, suggests extreme or violent events and upheavals that may affect those in power. Expect violent power struggles.

In Washington, D.C., the focus will be on all foreign relations in December 2002. Additional issues include finance, international hostilities, and continued focus on loss of life. Areas of concern may include countries in southern Africa, as well as Australia.

The solar eclipse of May 30, 2003, occurs at 9 degrees Gemini, and shows some localized stress in the Middle East. There could be problems with the leaders of these nations, as well as possible continued violence in Afghanistan.

---

4. This eclipse affects his Second and Eighth Houses, and contacts his Moon.

Did the Perpetrators Use Astrology?

Kris Brandt Riske

Evidence to date points to Osama bin Laden and his disciples of terror as responsible in part, if not in whole, for the September 11 attacks on the United States. Although the surviving terrorist planners failed miserably to cover their tracks after their murderous deeds, those who planned and carried out the events did so with studied knowledge of everything from security lapses at airports to the best time to drive large airliners into 110-story skyscrapers.

It was long ago when it was revealed that Nancy Reagan consulted an astrologer to plan the best times for her president-husband to meet with certain people or carry out certain functions. Timing is an essential ingredient in astrology.

Did the gang of terrorists practice astrology, check horoscopes, or consult astrologers at any stage in their plot? After studying a horoscope for the beginning of the September

11, 2001 terrorist attacks,[1] an astrologer, based on the partial success of the mission, could find evidence of the possibility that the attacks were planned and timed according to astrology. On the other hand, "polytheistic" astrology is forbidden in the Muslim faith.

Islam Web says that from an Islamic perspective, astrology is divided into two branches: polytheistic and lawful.[2] Polytheistic astrology, Muslim ruling states, "claims knowledge of the unseen . . . when such knowledge is unique to Allah." Muslims are not allowed to learn or teach polytheistic astrology because the Prophet regarded it as a branch of magic. Lawful astrology, Islam Web states, is the same as astronomy, in that it can help determine the times for prescribed prayers and other religious duties."[3]

In an article titled "The Concept of Destiny in Islamic Astrology and Its Impact on Medieval European Thought," the author laments that Western scholars have largely ignored astrology, and "the role of astrology in the Islamic world has also been ignored by western scholars, an oversight which is surprising in view of European astrologys' direct descent from Islamic sources."[4]

In summation, the article states, "For philosophers and theologians [astrology] offered something which Islam possessed but eleventh and twelfth century Christianity lacked

---

1. Flight 175 was the first plane to depart from an airport gate. The departure occurred on September 11, 2001, at 7:58 A.M. EDT in Boston, Massachusetts.

2. www.islamweb.net/english.

3. Ibid.

4. *ARAM: The Journal for Syre Mesopotamian Culture*, Vol. 1, No. 2, Summer 1989, p. 281–89.

—the prospect of a reasonable and rational route to comprehending God's creation. In addition, it held out the seductive prospect of control over a natural world, which was otherwise chaotic and threatening."

Certainly, there exists a modern prejudice against astrology on cultural, ethnic, and religious grounds, and that includes Muslim doctrine, says Dr. Abu Ameenah Bilal Philips in a treatise titled "The Islamic Ruling on Horoscopes." He writes that not only is the practice of astrology forbidden in the Muslim religion, "visiting an astrologer or reading one's horoscope are also forbidden. Since astrology is mainly used for predicting the future, those who practice it are considered fortune tellers."[5]

Dr. Philips concludes, "Belief in astrology and the casting of horoscopes are in clear opposition to the letter and spirit of Islam. And any Muslim who allows astrological predictions to determine his actions, should seek Allah's forgiveness and renew his Islam."

Muslims in America have discounted Osama bin Laden's adherence to Muslim doctrine. Many of them say he is the antithesis of Islam, a man who interprets and twists Muslim rulings to suit his own vicious ends. There is no evidence at this writing, however, that bin Laden practices polytheistic astrology or consults astrologers or checks his horoscope, but modern Muslims, writes Islam Web, might overlook the subject, "unaware of the ruling of Astrology."[6] Were bin Laden familiar with Muslim rule on astrology, however, he

---

5. Dr. Abu Ameenah Bilal Philips, "The Fundamentals of Tawheed," www.islamweb.net/english/.

6. Ibid.

could be viewed as one who would take "lawful" astrology (i.e., astronomy) and use its findings to determine the best time for an attack on America, an attack he would view as a religious duty.

Electional Astrology

The branch of astrology that governs event timing is called electional. In essence, an astrologer sets up a horoscope for the start of a venture, such as an incorporation date, the start of a job, a store opening, a contract signing, or any life event that would benefit from a propitious beginning. Electional horoscopes are timed to the minute, whenever possible, or within a short time span.

Ethical astrologers, those who are committed to assisting people to become the best they can be, would never advise anyone on when and where to commit a crime, such as a bank robbery or a terrorist attack.

When astrologers study the horoscope of a past event, this question is sometimes asked: Does the horoscope reflect the events, or do the events reflect the horoscope? In other words, were the date, time, and place selected to ensure success in their mission? Or does the horoscope symbolically represent the events that occurred at that moment?

Sometimes astrologers study an event horoscope and come to the conclusion that the horoscope is "too good" to be coincidental; that considerable thought and study went into the timing of the event.

Is that true of the September 11, 2001, attack on America?

It is impossible to know with 100 percent certainty, but the horoscope erected for the time that Flight 175 took off from Boston does open up the possibility of an attack that was planned through astrology. Although there were three other flights and four crashes involved in the attack, Flight 175 represents the onset of all the attacks because it was the first plane to take off in the formation of what were to become explosive missiles, piloted by a suicide squadron.

Dominant in the horoscope for the departure time of Flight 175 is the element of luck (or good fortune), something any astrologer would incorporate into an election horoscope.[7] The horoscope also suggests the operation was clandestine.[8]

The most dramatic message of the Flight 175 horoscope is one of massive destruction by a foreign power or foreign nationals whose overall goal was to destroy the American status quo. If an astrologer did select the timing of the attacks and designed the schedule with that end in mind, the chart (election) had the necessary components to ensure success.[9]

In addition to destruction of massive buildings symbolic of the American way of life, the horoscope also reflects a primary goal of sudden economic reversal—an attack on

---

7. Jupiter conjunct the Midheaven, the highest and most prominent point in the horoscope.

8. Sun in the Twelfth House of secrets, and Neptune (planet of illusion) trine the Ascendant.

9. The Saturn/Pluto opposition (a configuration that occurs approximately every thirty years) has Mercury trine Saturn and sextile Pluto. The configuration represents the careful planning that went into the operation as well as that it centered on transportation. The Third/ Ninth House placement of Pluto and Saturn reflect transportation and foreigners. Mercury in the First House represents the hijackers. Pluto signifies terrorism.

capitalism.[10] The president might have been a target, along with Congress (the Capitol building) and the Cabinet (White House), but the horoscope shows no strong indicator of the Pentagon as a target. That would have been more likely had the hijackings occurred later in the day.[11]

The other dominant feature of the horoscope is the void-of-course Moon.[12] There is much debate among astrologers about the significance of this phenomenon, which occurs approximately a dozen times each month. Some cite a "void-of-course" Moon (a Moon that does not move toward a connection) to another planet as meaning "nothing will come of it," meaning the event in question. Others believe that a void-of-course Moon signifies an event that goes on without interference, and that it doesn't know when to stop. If an astrologer was involved in planning the

---

10. Saturn (brick and mortar) opposing Pluto (destruction), and Venus (money) opposing Uranus (sudden change). Venus also was sextile Saturn and trine Pluto and in the Eleventh House of goals. The Venus/Uranus opposition also represents the hijackers (Venus as ruler of the Libra Ascendant) and Uranus (airplanes).

11. Jupiter in the Tenth House of the president, Venus in the Eleventh House of Congress. The sign Leo also represents the president, and Venus in the Tenth House of goals is in Leo. Mars (military) would have been opposed by the Moon later in the day after the Moon entered Cancer. The Sun and Jupiter rule the Cabinet.

12. The Moon is void-of-course, between the times it makes its last aspect to another planet and when it moves into another sign. The Gemini Moon's last aspect was a trine to Uranus approximately eleven hours before Flight 175 departed. The Moon thus went void-of-course on September 10 and remained that way until later in the day on September 11, when it entered Cancer.

attack on America, he or she may have thought that the selection of a void-of-course Moon would aid its success. That would be true only up to a point, though, because the Federal Aviation Administration (FAA) grounded all flights as a precaution to prevent additional hijackings.

Religion, Land, and Oil

Jonathan Keyes

Since the attack on America, some have questioned the tenets of the Islamic faith as inherently dangerous and violent. Due to the actions of a few fundamentalist and militant Islamic terrorists, the entire religion has been branded as threatening to our way of life. Concepts such as jihad have scared many people into believing that Muslims are more aggressive than their Judeo-Christian counterparts. Nothing could be further from the truth.

In a speech given at the Washington Islamic Center on September 17, President Bush said, "These acts of violence against innocents violates the fundamental tenets of the Islamic faith. The face of terror is not the true face of Islam. That's not what Islam is all about. Islam is peace."[1]

---

1. Carlyle Murphy, "Exploring Islam and its Traditions," the Los Angeles Times-Washington Post Service. *The Oregonian*, September 19, 2001, A16.

Islam: The Religion

To understand Islam, the religion of Muslims, it is important to understand how it came to be and how it is practiced today. In A.D. 570, the future prophet of Islam, Muhammad, was born in Mecca. Muhammad grew to be a businessman who lived and worked in that area until the age of forty. Around A.D. 610, Muhammad received revelations from the Archangel Gabriel that would continue for twenty-three years. These revelations became the basis for the holy book of Islam, the Koran. Muhammad gathered together a group of followers who were persecuted in that region, and to escape the attacks, Muhammad and his followers left Mecca for Medina in 622. This is known as the *Hijra*, or exodus, and marks the consolidation of the first Muslim community. When they returned to Mecca, he and his followers helped establish Islam as a religion. Muhammad died around 632 at the age of sixty-three.

The Koran teaches a brand of faith devoted to the one God, Allah. The tenets of the faith are peace, mercy, and forgiveness. Islam means "peace," or, "the peace that arises from the submission to the will of Allah." The holy tradition that formed the Muslim faith was born out of the Judeo-Christian world, and Muslims include much of the Old Testament into their religion as well. Finally, Muslims believe that Allah has complete rule over their daily lives, but that each individual is accountable for their actions and that there will be a day of judgment similar to the one expressed in the Christian Church.

In modern times, militant and fundamentalist Islamic sects have risen throughout the Muslim world. These sects comprise only a small fraction of the total 1.2 billion people who practice Islam, however, like the religious fundamentalists in the United States, their political voice is often much louder than their small minority warrants. Many of these groups, including the Taliban in Afghanistan, believe in a strict interpretation of the Koran that limits the rights and freedoms of women, harsh punishments for crimes, and most controversially, a violent form of jihad against all its enemies.[2]

Jihad

Jihad is a powerful word in the American psyche because it connotes violent retribution against enemies of the followers of Islam. Some scholars of Islam believe that jihad refers more to the struggle to overcome the darker impulses of one's self; to struggle against the forces of evil that we harbor in our hearts. In a larger context, most scholars believe that similar to the Christian faith, the Koran permits fighting in self-defense, and to protect land and home.[3] But it also forwards strict laws against harming civilians. These

---

2. Jonathan Tilove, "Exploring the Arab World," Newhouse News Service, September 21, 2001.

3. Available online at http://iisca.org/knowledge/jihad/meaning_of_jihad.htm, and at www.ict.org.il/articles/jihad.htm.

tenets are ignored by the more fundamentalist sects who would accomplish their aims at any price. In fact, it has been noted that these fundamentalists even killed members of their own religion. Over 700 Muslims were killed in the combined attacks on the World Trade Center and the Pentagon.

At this time, when Pluto and Saturn are opposite each other in the sky, the darkest aspects of fundamentalist Islam have risen to the surface. Astrologically, Pluto is associated with intense power and deep underlying emotions that can sometimes be hateful and vengeful. Certain Islamic militants have merged their intense faith with their anger at the United States into a violent force capable of intense destruction. But, ultimately, Pluto is associated with the process of purification. As Pluto transits through Sagittarius (the sign associated with religious faith) many fundamentalist Muslims, including the Taliban, are trying to practice what they see as the purest, most devout form of Islam. This purification process manifests itself in the form of jihad, a holy war against all Jews and against the United States.[4]

Of course, the movement of Pluto through Sagittarius affects people of all religions, and it is likely that religious fundamentalism and intolerance will rise to the surface throughout the world. We have already seen this in the

---

4. Barry Bearak, "Pakistanis, But Not Many, Angrily Take to the Streets to Denounce Bush's Stand," *New York Times,* September 22, 2001, B3. John F. Burns, "The Taliban: Clerics Answer 'No, No, No!' And Invoke Fates of Past Foes," *New York Times*, September 22, 2001, B3.

United States where Christian fundamentalists have expressed their belief that the attack on America was partly the fault of secularism (or a lack of pure religious faith) among feminists, the ACLU, pagans, and abortionists. Though these beliefs have been widely criticized by many people, including conservative Christians, it is apparent that religious intolerance is not restricted to a few Muslims.

Looking to the Past: The Crusades

Since its inception in the seventh century, the Muslim faith has grown and expanded until it has reached all corners of the globe. At certain times in history, conflict and strife have risen between followers of Islam and Judeo-Christian groups. One has to look back to the time of the Crusades to gain understanding of the conflict that exists today. Over nine hundred years ago, in 1076, Turkish Muslims had conquered the Christian Byzantine armies and went on to capture Palestine and Jerusalem.

The capture of Jerusalem horrified the Christian world and galvanized a set of European Crusades to retake the land that would last two hundred years. Islam, Judaism, and the Christian Church view Jerusalem as holy land. For the Muslims, a beautiful dome (the Dome of the Rock) was built on the site where Muhammad was said to have died. For Christians, Jerusalem was the site of Christ's crucifixion, making it the most holy place on Earth.

During the Crusades, armies of soldiers, peasants, and even children traveled overland from Europe to try and retake the holy lands. For over two hundred years Muslim and Christian armies exchanged ownership, until 1291, when

Muslim armies removed the last vestiges of European and Christian dominance in the region.[5]

Israel and Jerusalem: Site of Holy Battleground

Today, over seven hundred years after the time of the Crusades, the name of these wars alone is enough to reanimate ancient fears and hatreds. In modern times, anger has been focused on the Jewish peoples and their creation of Israel as a nation in 1948. Many secular and fundamentalist Muslims have been angered by the Israeli occupation of Arab territories since 1967.

The last time Pluto and Saturn were opposing each other was in 1965 and 1966. In 1967, the surrounding countries of Syria, Lebanon, Jordan, and Egypt geared up for an attack on Israel. However, Israel pre-empted with an attack of its own, taking the Gaza Strip, Golan Heights, and West Bank, including eastern Jerusalem. (They already controlled western Jerusalem.) Eastern Jerusalem is the site of the Muslim holy Dome of the Rock where Muhammad is thought to have ascended to heaven. This dome was also built on the site of the holiest temple of the Jews, of which only the Wailing Wall remains. Since the Six-Day War, Muslims throughout the world have been angered at Israeli control over their sacred religious site, as well as their occupation of Palestinian lands, where over a million Arabs live.[6]

---

5. www.csd.k12.wi.us/CRUSADES.HTM.
6. Information about the Six-Day War is available online at www.yahoodi. com/peace/sixdaywar.html.

Each of the occupied territories that Israel has taken over has been host to numerous terrorist organizations bent on freeing these lands from Israeli control, as well as destroying the Israeli nation. Terrorist organizations have developed in the surrounding Arab countries with similar aims. Many of the tactics of these terrorist organizations spring out of a strict fundamentalist Islamic interpretation of the Koran, which differs markedly from the more moderate approach of the majority of Muslim peoples in Arabic countries. Some of these terrorist groups include cells that are linked to bin Laden and his al Qaida organization.[7]

Since the creation of Israel in 1948, the United States has provided military, financial, and moral support to their government. Much of the anger Arabs direct toward Israel is also aimed at the United States. Since its inception, Israel has been in a state of constant vigilance, fearing military and terrorist attacks against its people. With the advent of the World Trade Center destruction, the United States now shares these fears.[8]

Astrological Interpretation of the Nation of Israel

To understand the current situation, it is helpful to look at the astrological chart of the birth of Israel as a nation.[9] In

---

7. Available online at www.antipas.org/daily.
8. See Jonathan Keyes, "All Eyes On Osama bin Laden," in this book for more information about bin Laden's position regarding the United States.
9. Available online at Lois Rodden's AstroDataBank at www.astrodata-bank.com/NMIsraelState.htm.

Israel's chart we find numerous telling features that explain Israel's nature. Israel has its Sun in Taurus, which accurately represents her steadfast nature and perseverance. Israel has been able to withstand the continual onslaught of terrorism and military attacks on all sides of its borders, which is also indicative of Taurus. Other astrological indicators describe Israel's sometimes intense and warlike nature.[10] With provocation, Israel will lash out and defend itself from incursion or threat.

Israel's chart also has a close association of Saturn and Pluto. Like the Pluto/Saturn relationship that is happening now, the formation in Israel's chart has to do with transformation of structure.[11] Israel, through its creation out of previously Arab dominated lands, has transformed the structure of the world around it. It has also transformed the arid desert into arable land (about 17 percent of Israel is arable land and about 1,800 square kilometers are irrigated[12]), and burgeoning cities, like Tel Aviv. As Israelis have transformed the structure of the land, they have also engendered deep hatred from the Arabs who live in nearby countries, or in the occupied territories that Israel took in 1967.

---

10. For example, Israel has Sun square Mars in its chart. Mars is associated with war in astrology.

11. Pluto is associated with transformation and Saturn with structure. In times of opposition, like the present, forces outside of oneself or one's country are usually causing the transformation; while in conjunctions (as in Israel's birth chart) the transformation is happening on an internal level.

12. *U.S. CIA World Factbook 2001* is available online at www.odci.gov/cia/publications/factbook/index.html.

Israel will now have to walk a fine line between defending their lands and offering appeasement to the Arabs who demand justice and the return of their lands. This is especially difficult when there are certain factions of Arab and Palestinian people who want nothing less than the complete destruction of Israel. Somehow, both the Middle Eastern countries and Israel have to find a middle way that allows for all peoples to live in those lands in peace. In previous peace accords, Israel and members of the occupied territories have agreed to share control over portions of the land. This is indeed the best solution, and one that would appease all except the most militant. Unfortunately, militant and fundamentalist religious groups from both the surrounding Arab countries and Israel have fought to defeat a compromise.

The Gulf War

From questions of religion and land, we move to questions of oil and economics. In late 1989, as the former Soviet Union was pulling out of Afghanistan, an army of soldiers from Iraq, under the command of Saddam Hussein, entered the small, oil-rich country of Kuwait. In January 1990, the United States launched an attack that would repel Iraq from Kuwait, killing thousands of Iraqi troops and civilians in the process.

Whether our interest in the Gulf was oil-based or an act of global policing, the effect of the war has been long lasting. Through aerial bombing, much of Iraq's infrastructure was reduced to ruins and precious sources of potable water and supplies of food were destroyed. In the aftermath of the war and during the long embargo afterwards, thousands, if not hundreds of thousands, of people died for lack of proper food, water, and medicine.

Two key factors have contributed to Muslim anger over the Gulf War—especially militant, fundamentalist Muslim anger. One of the key factors listed by bin Laden in his anger towards the United States is the stationing of foreign troops in his home country of Saudi Arabia. The other factor is the immense loss of life that took place in Iraq, with many of the casualties being civilians.

Finally, though, the United States repelled the Iraqi invaders and President George Bush Sr. made the choice not to take over Baghdad and eliminate Saddam Hussein. Hussein plays an important role in the crisis today. Though the current battle centers around bin Laden, it is likely to move towards the old conflict between the United States and Iraq. To understand the conflict and what may lie in store, it is helpful to look at Saddam Hussein's chart.[13]

Saddam Hussein's Chart[14]

Astrological factors show someone who is both stubborn and steadfast, and erratic and unpredictable, at once.[15] Hussein repeatedly defied the United States, sending his 500,000-man army up against the technologically superior American forces during the Gulf War. His chart also shows someone who is fierce and strong willed, someone who is willing to

---

13. Bernard Lewis, "Muslim Militants Reveal Different View of the World," *The Oregonian*, September 16, 2001, A14.

14. Saddam Hussein's birth data is from Lois Rodden's AstroDataBank at www.astrodatabank.com/ NMHusseinSaddam.htm

15. Saddam Hussein has his Sun and Uranus conjoined in Taurus.

fight.[16] This combination of factors makes him a dangerous man to tangle with. He is not likely to back down in any conflict, and he is likely take extreme measures to gain victory.

Oil

One of the main reasons Hussein invaded Kuwait was to secure the rich oil fields that they owned. Oil is at the heart of American economic weakness. Without oil, America and much of the Western world would literally grind to a standstill. Planes, automobiles, and trucks would be unable to run; the global economy would fall into disarray. The Middle East owns vast reservoirs of oil, which they sell throughout the world. During the 1970s, a consortium of Arab oil companies banded together to create OPEC. When OPEC decided to limit their supplies of oil, America experienced vast shortages that led to an oil crisis.

In our defense of Kuwait, we also wanted to ensure that oil fields would be owned and operated by friendly governments, even if they were not democratically elected and were often tyrannical, as in the case of Saudi Arabia. This conflict with bin Laden points to a deeper conflict over the ownership and trade of oil. If Hussein gets involved in this conflict, and I believe he will, the issue of oil will likely become a renewed area of concern.

Conclusion

In our campaign to rid the world of terrorists, it can be difficult to see the underpinnings of this attack. Some have

---

16. Hussein's Moon/Mars conjunction is in Sagittarius.

chosen to brand Islam a dangerous religion, when, in fact, only a small percentage of fanatics choose to interpret Islam in a violent and vengeful way. It is also important to see the attacks in the context of an ancient history of struggle encompassing the crusades up to the creation of Israel, and to the Gulf War. Issues of religious and cultural differences, territorial concerns, and a fight over oil supplies is also part of the equation.

In this time of the Saturn/Pluto opposition, these issues are all getting retriggered, and it is likely that the context in which we understand these issues will change in the near future. The United States is going through a crisis and a rebirth.[17] This is a time when our character and our belief systems will be changed and have to go through a growing process. If Americans chooses to reach out and understand our foreign neighbors better,[18] then there is the possibility for better relations and a lessening of conflict. Though some believe only war is called for, it is essential that we embark on a process of dialogue with other countries as well. It is also essential that we watch out for religious intolerance that would harm Arab-Americans in our own country. We do not want the same kind of religious intolerance that fundamentalists demonstrate.

---

17. This is signified by Pluto and Saturn transiting the United States Ascendant and Descendant. The Declaration of Independence was given at 5:10 P.M., 1776, in Philadelphia, Pennsylvania, and that is the chart I use here. There are other charts for the United States, but I have chosen this one because it seems to be the most accurate.

18. Foreign neighbors are represented by the Seventh House. This is where Saturn is transiting, and what Pluto is opposing in the United States chart.

Saturn and Slow Market Periods

Georgia Anna Stathis

E ven though we are entering a slow market period, it is important to remember that careful research and conservative investments are appropriate now. There is good news, though, for when this cycle completes, we will see a very healthy market activity, starting in 2003.[1] The healthy market activity will grow from the death of old structures and systems in management and investment. This process requires patience. Discoveries will reveal themselves in time, with research and study. The slower market and research period is operative between 2001 and 2002. The changes will involve banking, investment, taxation, interest rates, reconstruction, nuclear energy, and research and development.

---

1. Jupiter enters Virgo on August 28, 2003, and starts supporting the mutable Mars in all the charts explored in this piece.

Future Trends

Let's take research and development as an example of future change and potential investment opportunity. In the marketplace of quick and easy solutions, research and development was reduced early in the process of corporate retrenchment. In addition, senior employees were laid off because they were considered too expensive and too old. The corporate philosophy was to hire the young, hungry MBAs for $30,000 a year and get their money's worth. Expect to see a reversal of this trend as senior executives—research and development people—are brought back to work.[2] Wisdom is back in style. The realization that experience and knowledge count for a lot may be one of the major changes we see during the next two years.

The planet Saturn reflects slow and cautious activities along the lines of regrouping, recycling, and resourcefulness. The current environment that finds Pluto in a harsh relationship to Saturn suggests that our challenge is to move out of our fixed and known structures of business and investments and move slowly and surely in new ways of transacting business. We need to get lean and look at the long-term plan. The United States chart shows that the public isn't going to return to the spending habits of the time prior to September 11, that they are returning, instead, to the basics of living. This will create problems in the retail sales market as shoppers buy more of what they need, and less of what they want.

---

2. Saturn reflects senior (elder) status, and Pluto reflects regeneration.

Real Estate

Reduced spending suggests a strong possibility of changes in availability and value of real estate. Saturn reflects the building and vacant real-estate market. Reduced spending will lead to additional layoffs, and to a higher vacancy rate in real estate *if* the landowners do not alter the way they do business. If a business income is not meeting its expected monthly budget requirements, this suggests that those buildings will soon be empty.

As is always the case when Pluto is involved in a configuration with Saturn, we have a choice. We can keep doing things the way we always have and refuse to change, or we can get creative so that we survive. The San Francisco Airport provides an excellent example. After the recent attack, business fell off in the newly designed shops. Rather than lose tenants, the airport chose to charge the merchants a percentage of their sales rather than the fixed rents stated in their leases. This was an excellent "outside the box" solution that reflects strategic flexibility.

The housing market has risen sharply over the course of the last two years. Even with layoffs, there is still a need for housing, and prices are still high. To encourage home buying, reducing interest on mortgages is an important strategy. The mortgage rates had already dropped about nine times in the last year to encourage spending, but look for additional cuts to occur. It is quite conceivable that the mortgage rates could drop down to about 4.5 percent to continue stimulation of the housing market.

There will probably be an increased vacancy factor in rentals, and this makes it possible to negotiate very reasonable leases on rental property—commercial or residential.

People want to reduce spending.[3] This turning point is similar to frozen investment periods, which occur every seven years,[4] but with the added challenges created by terrorism, this trend will be accentuated even more.

Foreign Trade

An example of what we can expect has already occurred. Saudi Arabia is supportive of the United States in the current crisis, but they were careful in the beginning of the negotiations not to offer the Americans military bases in their country. They offered air space over which the American Air Force could fly, and they were vocal about their decision to disassociate themselves from the Taliban. However, in an interview on one of the BBC channels in London, their prime minister explained that they didn't feel comfortable offering military bases because Saudi Arabia was a Muslim country, and he felt they had to be very careful about alienating themselves from other Muslim nations. In other words, the issue of boundaries is a major factor in international relations. The Saudis find themselves in a kind of Catch-22. They are Muslims, but do not want to be associated with Taliban Muslims. How does one separate these two confusing issues? This is a difficult challenge that may

---

3. Saturn reflects limitation in people's thinking. With Saturn connecting to Mars in the charts we are considering, the suggestion is a lack of willingness to continue to pay high prices. Entire companies may relocate to less expensive locations, thereby developing new centers of business.

4. Saturn completes one-quarter of its cycle every seven years, thereby creating a challenging configuration by squaring its own position.

peak and reach the need for a solution in the summer of 2002.[5]

Since Saturn will stress Mars in the United States' chart throughout 2002, we face a market that is very flat and moves sideways for at least for two years. It suggests choices that include more reliable investments such as hedge funds, long-term growth funds, and, of course, the strategy here might be to buy while prices are low because spending and investment appear to be rather slow in the New York Stock Exchange' chart.[6]

It is important to remember that this recessionary cycle had already begun before September 11. It was inevitable that there would be a slow down. But the attack exacerbated the problem tenfold. The sudden changes triggered difficulties in the money flow and money cycle. New economies are coming in and old economies are exiting as things turn. The shock of the decline of the tech sector is still with us with fallout continuing in an increasing unemployment rate as well as decreased investor interest in this area.[7]

The low numbers in the market suggest that things are dying out, but as a cycle dies, there is always another cycle moving forth toward a new future.[8]

---

5. In the middle of 2002, Saturn is in the late degrees of Gemini conjuncting the United States Mars (1776) at 22 degrees of Gemini.

6. Using May 17, 1792, for 12 P.M. in New York, New York.

7. In the New York Stock Exchange chart, transiting Uranus is hitting natal Pluto at 23 Aquarius 31. Uranus is volatile and this continues through 2001 and a portion of 2002.

8. This is indicated by the fact that transiting Saturn, throughout the year, is hitting the NYSE chart Mars in the First House of identity, which is usually aggressive in its movements. Mars is the ruler of the Eighth House, which represents support from others like investors.

The New Economy

The new economy, still in its formation stages, is a meta-morphosis of technology and biology. The new economy is biotech, and it is shown not only in the New York Stock Exchange chart, but also by many upcoming planetary combinations.[9]

In 2002 and 2003 we can expect to see strangers and strange new developments.[10] Can it be that some unexpected alliances may form or change around China? Is it possible that some sort of alliance or assistance, or even a breaking down of the Communist structure in China could begin to occur? Such changes will dramatically affect our markets, possibly enlarging our financial alliances.

Additional indicators connected with Uranus and Neptune include economy possibilities such as more mergers between airlines, which may become collectively owned by either government or countries. This change might be spurred by their recent difficulties and restrictions.[11] Watch for a shift in science and technology, particularly in the energy field where electricity and chemicals combine to create new types of energy sources, such as fuel cells. Newly emerging sciences stem from combining chemicals with fluids of the body,

---

9. Uranus will be entering Pisces, reflected by Neptune, in a couple of years and this combination can cross over between technology and liquids of the body such as blood and DNA. Neptune is already in Aquarius, similar to a Uranus/Neptune conjunction.

10. Uranus, which signals strangers, is transiting the same degree in which Neptune was discovered, during March, April and December of 2002.

11. Saturn is associated with restrictions, and it will be in Gemini, the sign associated with transportation.

like blood combined with DNA, and become jumping-off points.[12] This captures and pursues diseases at the root level. Pay particular attention to the research that has been going on in the Genome Project and genetic engineering, which began in the last two years. The current research on stem cells, as a source for healing birth defects and diseases, is on the cutting edge, as are the new possibilities of responsible cloning. The discovery of the structure of DNA in recent years is aligned with the current transit of Uranus over the discovery position of Neptune.

Invention and Energy

Uranus characterizes electricity. Is it possible that nerve damage could be solved by designing some sort of liquid electricity that cauterizes the damaged nerve endings, or, in fact, fertilizes them with a DNA cocktail that promotes growth, or, at least, temporary relief that ultimately leads to more permanent solutions. Since Uranus describes electricity as well as networks, electrical networks in homes or neighborhoods may become a reality. Rather than just having a computer network in your office or home, perhaps a digital type of cable that is cooperative in nature could supply the needed electricity to run appliances in homes and buildings at a more affordable cost.

A new focus on the sea and water as new sources of energy is inevitable. The current energy crisis for gas and electricity is a harbinger for other natural resources such as our water supply. New types of energy result from inventions

---

12. Neptune and Uranus are related to discoveries concerning DNA.

that create waterpower, or, even make water. If animals and plants can be cloned, why can't we develop new water supplies? We could awaken to a need for more energy-efficient water processing plants, water storage structures, dams, and hydraulics. The transport of water energy and water supply could also develop. This increase in water accessibility leads to new and different methods employed in agricultural growth such as hydroponics, or even vertical farms—hydroponics farming in structures several stories high.

We are seeing all types of appliances being designed to be more energy efficient, with energy companies contributing large rebates for individuals to take advantage of these opportunities. This reduces demand for electrical or gas energy and saves money.

Communications

Wireless communications, the Internet, and more sophisticated, refined video conferencing will help to resolve new limitations in air travel. The problems associated with flying may actually be the impetus for development of more refined technological systems that will provide virtual meetings that rival in-person meetings. This change also reduces gas costs and energy costs. The amalgamation of cell phones into multipurpose devices that send and receive messages, videoconference, track travel plans, keep notes, and fax may provide the new magic wands of the twenty-first century.

Communication equipment, particularly computers, are getting smaller and smaller. We are seeing smaller keyboards and televisions; and the fusion of several pieces of equipment in one.[13]

Information Media

In a recent (September 2001) television interview, Walter Cronkite, one of the most well-respected journalists of our time, encouraged the government to form a security task force of information censors. The purpose of this board would be to temporarily hold back information on current military tactics and strategy from the media in order to assure secrecy and success in military missions. All information would be saved and released in its entirety after the military operations take place. In this way we maintain our freedom of speech rights as a nation, but do not reveal too much information in the beginning of the maneuvers.

This freezing of information is also reflected in the freezing of funds. The United States must be more cautious about financial concerns, dispensing funds carefully in the form of aid and loans. Recently, an electronic freeze on funds in bank accounts of known terrorist networks was wisely implemented, and a universal warning that no funds will be distributed for those who support the terrorist network in anyway was timely.

New Forms Emerge

New forms of publishing and publication formats are past due. We may see smaller magazines, smaller books, and

---

13. Saturn indicates the smaller size, Gemini the communication, and Pluto the fusion of several things into one.

more acceptance for electronic publishing than in the past because of the current energy crisis and resource shortages.

The building industry may experience changes as basic building methods, such as the new clear concrete that is being used by architects in building designs.[14] Contemporary designs of infrastructure show through the new clear concrete. This is a completely different concept in the visual look of buildings. Building buildings within buildings, or underground, is also possible. After the recent World Trade Center attack, it seems that one would build important centers downward rather than upward. In fact, building materials codes could stringently change with Saturn in opposition to Pluto.

Since Saturn rules building as well as the rules/codes, and Saturn (form and structure) is opposing Pluto (transformation), the idea of eliminating toxins from buildings and the building process may finally take hold. After years of fighting the invisible toxins such as asbestos, molds, and mildews, people might actually get relief from substances that cause severe health problems.

Changes in Health Care

Saturn symbolizes skin, bones, and teeth, which are also structures. We may see a major change in the orthopedic industries as well as the dental and dental supply industries. New surgical techniques that require fewer incisions

---

14. The Saturn/Pluto combination we see now suggests new building styles and materials.

have been on the increase in medical technology over the last few years. A new direction may be to inject cultured cartilage instead of resorting to surgery.

Another new technique may come in the form of patches on the skin. For years now, people have been excellent results with nicotine patches to aid them in quitting smoking. Drug companies are also perfecting birth control patches. And the idea of using patches for various deficiencies in the body's cartilage system, collagen system, or adrenal system may be on the cutting edge of change. We may finally see advancements in treatment for highly allergic patients whose allergies are trigger by environmental factors, too.[15]

Either newly refined laser technologies will increase over the course of the next two years, or liquids that are injected, or absorbed from patches attached to the skin may be designed to increase the mobility of those hampered with joint disease, particularly arthritis, and calcium deficiencies that destroy body structure.

Conclusion

On September 11, 2001, the United States was confronted with a catastrophe—we lost our childhood and entered adulthood. We were forced to grow up and begin the process of rebuilding. This tragedy, directed toward destroying our country, backfired. Ironically, the terrorists' actions brought forward the courage, heroism, and ethics upon which our

---

15. Saturn rules the skin, and Gemini rules the hands, arms, shoulders, and lungs.

society was founded for re-examination. On that day we began democratic adulthood, and what seemed to be our darkest hour was the beginning of our future—because there is always a future. No longer can we foolishly say, "It can't happen here," because it did.

Recommended Reading

The New New Thing: A Silicon Valley Story by Michael Lewis (Penguin Group: 2001).

Strategy, Spending, and the Planet Mars

GEORGIA ANNA STATHIS

For astrologers, Mars represents spending and the motivation behind spending. Mars reflects two things in the economy: wars and investments, or in other words, strategy and spending. There are three ways the energy of the war/investment cycle can go:

- Assertive, even aggressive effort—kick down doors by force, or scouting for new directions;

- Fixed or sustained effort—hold the line, and finish what the first group started; and

- Flexible, moveable effort—constant, quick movements that reflect sudden insights and quicksilver solutions.[1]

---

1. Astrologers recognize three kinds of energy—cardinal, mutable, and fixed. Aries, Cancer, Libra, and Capricorn are the cardinal signs; Taurus, Leo, Scorpio, and Aquarius are the fixed signs; and Gemini, Virgo, Sagittarius, and Pisces are the mutable signs.

It is in this third category that we find a high percentage of the motivational energy in most of the charts we are considering in this book. Here the greatest strength, as well as the greatest weakness, lies in the ability to be flexible enough to bend with circumstances, and to connect the right people with the right solutions. This ability to connect quickly is challenging because focus can be a problem. So many opportunities or ideas may develop that we get too many irons in the fire.[2] Staying focused is the ultimate challenge here. We find Mars, the spending symbol, in the flexible mode in both the New York Stock Exchange (NYSE) and NASDAQ charts.[3] Both charts reflect the recent markets where we have experienced investment success. The flexible mode is also suited to the American temperament of changeability, youthfulness, flexibility, and trying new things.

The ability to poll others for potential solutions and to bring together many details and philosophies reflects Mars placement in a mutable (flexible) sign, showing a highly developed problem solving skills. However, investment requires a plan, and that takes time, resources, and energy to make it as efficient as possible. The skill is flexibility; the result is intelligent action. Like the martial art of aikido, mutable movement fights the attacker by responding in a point/counterpoint fashion. In other words, when an action is taken, rather than reacting, the defender steps aside and out of the way of the aggressor until the aggressor has

---

2. Mars is associated with both iron and fire.

3. Mars is in Sagittarius in the NASDAQ chart, and in Virgo in the New York Stock Exchange chart.

fully committed his or her energy. Then the defender takes action to subdue the opponent.

Mars in the flexible mode is also like a cobra that dances with its enemy. It remains suspended, waiting for its target to tire or retire. The entire time the cobra is constantly assessing the situation. It strikes, if necessary, when least expected. This is the strategy that the United States employed in its response to the September 11 attack, and is also what many of the companies and markets are doing to combat the recession.

Recession Reality

A business recession was already on its way before September 11, but it was thrust upon us, creating a more immediate entrance into difficult economic times. When we look at the NYSE and NASDAQ charts, we find that Mars (spending and the motivation behind investing) is in a state of freeze over the course of the next two years.

There are two things to emphasize about the present situation:

- We were already heading into a recession and the resultant slowdown in spending and investment that occurs roughly every seven to eight years; and

- The recession is more intense because of other factors that are reflected in the planetary cycle landscape.[4]

---

4. See Georgia Anna Stathis, "Saturn and Slow Market Periods," in this book for more information about the effects of Saturn and slowdown periods.

Before the attack of September 11, the markets were already pushing plateau levels and resistance. For example, the Dow Jones Industrial Average, since the beginning of the year, couldn't break past the 10,000 to 11,000 levels. On January 31, 2001, it was at 10,887; then continued through late February at 10,495; then dropped to 9,878 in March; rose slightly to 10,734 in April; and then to 10,911 in May, where it started wavering. Currently, at this writing, it is at 9,060.[5]

Online Investing

The flexible way people have been investing online in the last few years is suited to the American marketplace. However, this new and changeable factor has thrown a monkey wrench into the more traditional and seasoned systems of investing through brokers and clearing houses. The truth is that many uneducated and unknowledgeable people got in the marketplace and were jumping in and out, contributing to recent market volatility. The fluctuations resulting

---

5. Mars went retrograde at 29 degrees Sagittarius on May 11, 2001, which usually restricts or cautions people on spending. In addition, it reached a very critical degree in that this was the opposite degree of the upcoming total solar eclipse of June 22, 2001, at 00 degrees Cancer. 29 degrees Gemini. Polaris, the pole star, or North Star, is located at 00 degrees Cancer. Polaris is used for navigating. If you are lost, then you look for the Pole Star to find your way home. Ironically, this is a metaphor for what is happening. We feel lost and are looking for a solution. The recent total eclipse at this position suggests that the navigation of our global concerns is at a turning point and we are in the shadow of the eclipse. We can't quite see our way out of the darkness, but are guaranteed that we will emerge from it because there is a future light for all eclipses.

from the entrance of new "dot coms" into the market have applied pressure to the old market model of investing and spending.[6]

In addition, the burgeoning tech field has dominated a high percentage of the investment markets over the last few years. This field is highly favored by the fluctuating, fickle indicators of the moveable and flexible Mars type. Things kept moving at a very fast pace, juggling quickly as they moved forward. We see many factors that exacerbated the already volatile behavior of the investment Mars in the charts for the United States, NASDAQ, and NYSE. Some incredible portfolios of massive amounts of communication, telecommunication, and e-business stock holdings were produced, and they found a perfect bedmate with the charts of the United States and the American markets, where heaven is a phone, a car, and a wireless computer.[7]

Economic Winter

A frozen economic winter has descended upon us earlier than might have been expected, however, because of the economic blast of the World Trade Center attack. Up front, this suggests a very hard and flat market for at least two years, that will have the appearance of nongrowth and of no insight into what might be better choices for investments. Without sounding too metaphorical, winter is always an

---

6. The planet Saturn reflects the old market model—a structured model of carefully paced spending.

7. The planet Mars is in Virgo in the NYSE chart, and in Sagittarius in the NASDAQ chart. Mars in Gemini in the United States chart suggests all these flexible communication devices.

amazing season. Though it seems that things are frozen—
we even wonder why we bother to prune our trees—in the
spring lots of new growth appears as a reward. The greater
the pruning in the winter, the greater the growth when the
season is ready for it. This is the tenor of our market and
economy right now.[8]

The energy in the terrorist attack chart indicates the
first kind of energy I have explained—the aggressive, forceful kind. It shows action that requires defensive measures
that were not in place at the time of the attack. The lack of
preparedness shows the need for more highly developed intelligence and security operating systems. This includes refined security devices that will instantly (mutable) analyze
details and patterns of eye scans, head or face scans, and
detailed bar codes generated at check-in. The bar code could
be attached to tickets, baggage, or even the body of the passenger (through some sort of indelible ink), whereby that
passenger is tracked throughout the airport security system
as he or she embarks on their journey.[9] This same technology can also be used for all the employees of the airports,

---

8. The attack of the terrorist network hit us just as the symbol of aggression and motivation, Mars, returned to the point in the zodiac where
   it had receded to in mid-May 2001 at almost 00 degrees Capricorn,
   and where the Dow Jones was then hitting about 10,900. Another
   strong impact is the fact that Mars had just crossed the Galactic Center. When planets cross the Galactic Center, things happen at warp
   speed—the future changes more rapidly than during normal cycles,
   creating sudden surprises and anxieties, which are not easily assimilated by human beings.

9. Instant response is associated with Mars, as are the head, face, and
   retinal blood vessels.

the security police, as well as the airline employees. It requires more sophisticated readings by computers and tremendous amounts of development money, but this technology will also assist in increasing intelligence and security measures for all industries, not only the airline industry.

In fact, one of the upcoming difficulties we may see is a new wave of white-collar crime. We have had forensics for crimes of murder for many years, wherein incredible amounts of information are assimilated, measured, and ultimately used to solve these crimes. Now, an entirely new security field of white-collar forensics and equipment could develop from this tragedy.

A Look at Some of the Astrological Charts

In the Bush inaugural chart,[10] Mars (war and aggression) is in the portion of the chart that reflects how others view us. In addition, it is stressfully positioned with a very volatile energy, suggesting sudden and out of the blue actions from others when we least expect it.[11] During the course of the next year, the inaugural chart suggests that there will be major confrontations between the United States and others, not only because of unexpected aggression upon us, but also some sort of financial limitation. In addition, this placement implies the need for sudden decisions concerning such

---

10. The inauguration chart is the birth moment of the new presidential term of office. See the chart list on page 255 for the chart data.

11. Uranus makes a square (90 degree aspect) to Mars between the Tenth House (public reputation) and the Seventh House (open enemies).

things as strategy and war, action and wounding, and an awakening to heroism.[12] Mars is in Scorpio in this chart, a sign that suggests the sustained effort we expect from the president and administration.

Looking at George W. Bush's birth chart, his natal Mars, the first planet to rise above the horizon (in the location he was born) after his birth, is in Virgo, one of the mutable signs. The sign of Virgo suggests the challenge of attending to many details, assessing the need for each choice, carefully assimilating, and then deciding which action to take to be most efficient. In addition, Mars in Bush's birth chart is associated with earning power, spending, and abilities that help him do the job that results in the most earning power.[13] This is also a marker known for spending and making money.

The current political situation has forced this administration to pick and choose with whom they will associate regarding financial concerns; and to be critical and clear about their choices as they set up systems to generate the support to fight the terrorist network.[14]

Mars reflects heroic times, heroic people, and heroic deeds. Heroism is a value we have reconnected during the

---

12. There is an 8 to 9 degrees difference in the square, which translates to eight to nine months after the inauguration. At this time Mars opposes Saturn in Taurus, indicating a financial problem.

13. Mars is in the Second House, the sector associated with material goals and money.

14. In looking at Bush's progressed chart, his progressed Sun is within three degrees of his natal Mars, pushing him to learn to discriminate and act strategically over the course of the next three years.

course of this tragedy. In fact, for some time we haven't had any real-life heroes. The actions of everyone closely involved in the terrorist attacks have sparked awareness of heroism in our country. This spark has returned us to the values of protecting and caring for each other.

The planet Mars reflects the "fight." The sign in which we find it shows us where the fight is directed. Virgo suggests a fight to strategize, or to protect against such things as new systems and methods, new security technologies, and health hazards. Mars in Scorpio reflects a sustained effort that ultimately transforms the way governments interact in the global drama.

In many ways, this new war is eclectic. It isn't just about attacking and fighting back with military power, but implementing all the modern technologies that we have at our disposal. In many ways this is a "cyber war" where we can freeze bank accounts, track records, track histories, send propaganda, send information on closed communication channels, and even use cyberspace to send out decoys. In other words, this is a war that is smarter and potentially quite different from previous conflicts.

Mars also represents that for which we have passion. For example, in the chart of the Taliban occupation of Afghanistan calculated for April 25, 1992, at 2:22 P.M. AFST in Kabul, Afghanistan, we see Mars in the Seventh House, again, the house of open enemies. It is in the sign of Pisces, symbolizing mysticism and faith, suggesting aggressive actions motivated by passion and religion. The interesting point here is that in the frenzy to destroy the "infidel," there is a conscious effort being made to mix up the beliefs of the

Taliban with the beliefs of Muslims. We hear in the news, over and over, that the United States is not fighting the Muslim faith, but the sect known as the Taliban, who claim they are also good Muslims. There is a mix-up here of terms. Mars in Pisces reflects the inability to set boundaries and terms, so confusion will continue to be a problem during this process.

Conclusion

Within a few hours of the attack, the New York Stock Exchange was closed.[15] Fears revolved around questions about how the markets would respond when they opened on Monday, September 17, 2001? On the first day, Monday, there was an amazingly small loss of less than 10 percent. As the week proceeded, we did see a very bad week, but, in comparison to what might have happened, it remained amazingly steady. Now we face a slow growth period. See the chapter on Saturn and Slow Market Periods for information about how this cycle is likely to develop.

---

15. In the chart of the New York Stock Exchange, Mars is in the same sign as Bush's chart—Virgo. On September 11, 2001, the transiting Sun (which lights up or burns out) hit the New York Stock Exchange Mars, closing the Stock Exchange within hours in a quick, Mars-like response.

A New Economy

GEORGIA ANNA STATHIS

W hether the perpetrators realized it or not, their intent to destroy the United States economy might be the action that sets this country, as well as the world, in a new direction toward cooperation among governments.[1] In addition, the intent of the attack was to destroy the "infidels," an action that backfired, as the tragedy ignited a dormant spirituality inherent in the Constitution of the United States ("one nation under God"). What was intended to separate, is uniting, particularly in the investment and commerce sector. The impetus of defense ultimately opens new economic territory.

The New Economic Scene

Before we start into a discussion about a new economy, it is important to define economy. Economy is the study of how

---

1. Libra and Capricorn, ruled by Venus (associated with alliances) and Saturn (associated with governments), opposing Pluto (associated with fusion), support this conclusion.

goods and services get produced and how they are distributed. The *how* includes thrifty management, frugality in expenditures and consumption of money, and management of resources.[2]

Different economic systems have developed, based on the values and philosophies of different nations. Some of the current economic models are capitalism, communism, and combined economies, where there might be more government control than straight capitalism, but not as much control by government as occurs in communism.

Communism may completely disappear by the year 2011, or, take on a new form more suited to the present economic times. In 2011, Neptune, which represents mergers and the breaking down of borders, is reaching the point in the zodiac where it was first discovered in 1846.[3] The concept of communism was concurrent with Neptune's discovery. To quote Geraldine Hatch Hanon in her book *Sacred Space*:

> "Not only was Neptune's discovery synchronistic with the emergence of the two major economic/political systems of this century, communism and capitalism, but its discovery announced the beginning of a cycle in which those oppressed by the white man's form of

---

2. The astrological interplay is between Mars and Saturn on the one hand, and Venus and Saturn on the other.

3. Neptune reflects imagination, healing, soul work, and spiritual faith on the positive side. It reflects the ability to visualize and then manifest. On the negative side Neptune reflects madness, depression, and excess use of drugs. As with all the planets, Neptune has its creative and destructive sides.

democracy were taking action in their struggle for freedom and equality. Since Neptune has a 165-year orbit, it has yet to return to its discovery position of 26 degrees Aquarius. Over the years, however, as it has made the dynamic aspects of either the square or opposition to its discovery position, these aspects have marked turning points in the evolution of communism, as well as in the rights of women and Blacks."[4]

In a time when borders and boundaries are rapidly changing, starting with the downfall of communism in the former Soviet Union in the late 1980s, we see new unions and alliances forming. The European Union has created a united currency called the Euro. The Internet reaches Germany as quickly as New Jersey. We have up-and-coming payment services, such as Pay Pal, that facilitate easy international payment. There is even a new word in the dictionary called *e-commerce*. The challenge here is that technology has moved us out of the box of the old economy and technology is ahead of the law. Another challenge is that goods, services, and information is crossing swiftly across state and country lines. One piece of equipment contains parts from several different countries, with the countries of origin listed on the labels.[5]

What does this kind of alliance suggest in terms of economic opportunities that the new global alliance against

4. Geraldine Hatch Hannon, *Sacred Space* (Firebrand, 1990).

5. These changes are coincident with Saturn square Uranus in July of 1999, November 1999, and May 2000, as well as Jupiter conjunct Saturn in May of 2000.

terrorism is reinforcing? It suggests that there will come a time, after we really learn how to negotiate, when we will consider new currencies that unify nations. We probably won't see this until 2021,[6] when a period unifying international business and economic networks is ushered in. We can expect changes in the entire field of currency, loan markets, extended payments, all-time low interest rates, and taxation, allowing freer exchange and breakthroughs in investment possibilities.

This new economy embraces prosperity while including new international partnerships that require a conscious exclusion of fear.[7] Conflicting philosophies and political views often generate fear in already faltering economies, because of the conflict of values.

Value in the form of tangible assets is the basis of any economy. This view may be outdated as a new value system emerges, and intangibles, such as knowledge, education, and powerful relationships in a highly sophisticated virtual environment take on importance. In an exclusive interview carried only in Financial Executives International online magazine, Barry D. Libert, coauthor of *Cracking the Value Code*, states, "Value, in the New Economy, is defined differ-

---

6. This is the time when Jupiter conjuncts Saturn in Aquarius.

7. Saturn reflects cold, slow, cautious action. Not only is it in a two-year stressful relationship with the spending planet, Mars, in all of the charts mentioned, including the inaugural chart of George W. Bush, but it is also positioned very stressfully with the transformative energy of Pluto. This cycle only occurs once every thirty-six or so years, and accompanies major political changes that result from clashes in political views.

ently than in all the previous economies. In the New [Economy], we create value with intangible assets such as people, relationships, property, patents, and prophecies. Historically, the way value was created and measured was with things and money. For the first time ever, starting around 1972, we saw a huge transition of value. And so the New Economy is older than just recently [simply Internet and technical companies], and it's changing the source of value".[8]

Recommended Reading

Cracking the Value Code by Barry D. Libert, Steve M. Samek, and Richard E. S. Boutlon (Harperbusiness, 2000).

The Essential Buffett: Timeless Principles for the New Economy by Robert G. Hagstorm (John Wiley & Sons, 2001).

---

8. Available online at www.fei.org/magazine, and link to FEI Online Exclusives.

The New Investment Climate

Georgia Anna Stathis

To determine the climate for spending, investment, and generally, the way things will go for the next quarter, astrologers use charts that mark the beginning of each season.[1] We can look at these in various ways. One simple way is to review positive influences versus challenges. We weigh the numbers to calculate the percentages in a consistent way each quarter.

General Economic Indicators

Both the fall and winter quarter invariable show the same stresses and anxieties as the indicators follow a seasonal pattern. It would be wise to reorganize portfolios and keep

---

1. Ingress charts are calculated for the moment a planetary body enters a sign. The most common ingress charts are the moments of seasonal shift cycles. These occur as the Sun enters Aries at 00 degrees at Spring Equinox, at 00 degrees Cancer at Summer Solstice, at Fall Equinox at 00 degrees Libra, and at 00 degrees Capricorn at Winter Solstice.

spending down from fall 2001 into 2002. But it's even more important to tackle this task as the summer quarter begins in 2002. In the second half of the summer quarter, beginning on June 22, 2002, we begin to see some recovery, even optimism. It is very important to note that the late part of July and all of August 2002 are not to be misinterpreted with overoptimism.

Fall quarter 2002 could initiate a period of false optimism, resulting in debt growth, or people rushing to get back on the investment wagon. Oil prices may stay at low levels throughout the this next year, but as fall 2002 begins, the price begins to climb, as do interest rates. However, it is clear, in looking at these charts, that interest rates are hitting a historical low to generate spending. The government may also offer tax breaks to further stimulate spending and business. Regardless, as the pall lifts in late summer 2002, it is important to stick with very stable and low-risk stocks at least for the next year. You can expect a more regular positive shift to occur in the marketplace in 2003.

The following is an overview for each quarter beginning with fall 2001. All charts were calculated for Washington, D.C.

Fall Quarter:
September 22, 2001, 7:04 P.M. EDT[2]

Price declines are highlighted in this quarter in order to generate spending. This theme continues throughout the winter quarter. There is great difficulty in traffic, communications, the postal services, or any courier or messenger service that is used to convey information. This limitation seeps over into Internet communications, traffic controller

information, licensing agreements, and may include a decline in exports. Buying is depressed. The real-estate market slows down tremendously. A high number of layoffs are
indicated in this chart that peak around October 5, 2001.
We are developing new partnerships with armed services in
the United States as well as abroad. Methods and systems
are highlighted for extreme change as truths are divulged
concerning the true level of financial securities.

Health difficulties are on the rise in this chart, with out-
breaks of various infectious diseases. Historically, during astrological periods like the present one, disease and plagues
have increased. William H. McNeill, author of *Plagues and
People*,[3] writes that the course of history was changed by the
rapid spread of disease over vast portions of the population,
thus changing powers and economics. Not only did disease
wipe out populations, but it also acted as a catalyst between
warring populations. Change was triggered when disease
prevented people from defending themselves and from attacking. For example, after driving the Spanish out of Mexico

---

2. Price declines are indicated by such things as (1) Mercury slowing
down before retrograde, (2) Mars in Capricorn; like Saturn, Mars'
placement in Capricorn restricts spending, and (3) Mars on South
Node makes the problem more difficult. The Saturn opposition Pluto
throughout the year suggests an environment of caution. Venus in
Virgo in the Sixth House and coming up to square Saturn on one side
and Pluto and the Moon on the other, indicates reduced money supply, no price increases, limited storehouses of wealth. This also suggests refinancing to try to consolidate debt. Infectious diseases are associated with the planets Pluto or Mars. Venus squares Pluto on
October 1 and the Moon on October 2, possibly indicating disease
problems. Venus, Pluto, and Mars are not favorably aspected in this
ingress chart.

3. William H. McNeill, *Plagues and People* (Anchor Books, Anchor Press,
Doubleday: 1976).

City, the man that organized the assault on Cortez fell prey to smallpox, as did his compatriots.[4] Since the Aztecs were unable to fight Cortez they were defeated. In addition, the more psychological side of this might have been that the Aztecs believed their gods had "let them down," thus opening the door to massive conversions to Christianity.

The Black Plague changed the course of England's history,[5] and disease was a major player in wiping out the Mesopotamian population following the Arab conquests of the seventh century A.D.[6] In a recent news article released by Stratfor[7] on October 5, 2001, reports that "an outbreak of an ebola-like virus has been reported on the Pakistan-Afghanistan border, raising concerns about biological warfare and dangers to U.S. troops. But while the disease could take a major toll on Afghan refugees, U.S. forces are not likely at risk."

Health concerns suggest an increased market demand for medicines, health preventative systems, and manufactured products and goods. Such a demand could be a positive outgrowth of this difficult situation. Since imports, public relations, and public information are highlighted in this chart, there could be a great deal of public information on prevention measures during the holiday season of 2001. Health education is essential for all citizens of the world.

---

4. This happened in 1519, and there was a Saturn/Pluto conjunction in 1518.

5. The plague began in 1348. There was a Saturn/Pluto conjunction in 1350.

6. The conquest concluded in 639, and there was a Saturn/Pluto square in 638.

7. Stratfor can be accessed online at www.stratfor.com.

Winter Quarter:
December 21, 2001, 2:23 P.M. EST

Frozen assets, borrowing, stock portfolios, and asset reorganization are highlighted this quarter. This suggests a good time to rework portfolios to be leaner, meaner, and risk averse. The stock market will be somewhat volatile during this time, particularly around December 11–15, as well as around December 27–31. The Federal Reserve may announce further cuts in interest rates to encourage people to stay in the markets.

This is likely to be an interesting time in the real-estate market. As mortgage rates decline, they may be the best deal in years. Watch for rapidly dropping real-estate values to provide more affordable housing, and some sort of tax break to homeowners. This might look like a government rebate on the purchase of a home, or, possibly, loan packages that are different from the standard V.A. or F.H.A. loans.

It looks as though sellers are eager to let go of homes too, suggesting a unseasonal buyers' market during the holidays. Housing, in general, drops in price for renters as well as homeowners. Renegotiating leases that are about to run out is a good strategy here since the vacancy rate is on the rise.

This unseasonal buyers' market crosses over into the retail sales divisions during the holidays. Selling goods at close to cost to unload the supply is not unthinkable, particularly near the Christmas holidays. Collaboration among merchants could result in a hybrid sales format in malls—a block sale, for example—to demonstrate a new spirit of alliance.

The largest factor in the Winter Ingress chart is the employment situation. The state of unemployment remains high throughout the fall and winter quarters as companies seek equilibrium, but this same state of unemployment is a fertile field for new and different services being offered by the technically astute unemployed. This next quarter may be an opportunity to apply your skills to transforming systems, work environments, and data base systems, so you can act as an independent, self-employed agent. The cracks in the corporate structures will require skillful analysis and interpretation by qualified independent contractors.

After January 18, 2002, this potential self-employment strategy becomes more prominent. The well-trained, unemployed individual could also be hired to do in-depth research to help create a better structure for your temporary boss that offers more seamless technical or environmental systems. For those who need training, this quarter offers great opportunities to pursue licensing opportunities or vocational training.

Spring Quarter: *March 20, 2002, 2:16 P.M. EST* [8]

Flash! A new WPA model (Work Projects in World War II) may form as the result of the unemployment situation in

---

8 Neptune, which rules the Eighth House (income) falls in the Sixth House (labor unions and negotiations) and aligns with the Seventh House (partnerships and new partnering possibilities). Mars, the ruler of the Ninth House (travel) is square Neptune (mergers) in the Sixth House. Also, Neptune, the ruler of the Eighth House, is in the Sixth House (employment) and trine the Moon in Gemini. The Moon rules the people and it is close to Saturn (struggle). Venus the ruler of the Third House (exports) placed in the Ninth House (foreign exports) suggests strength in this area of the economy. Additionally, Venus rules the Tenth House (manufactured product supply) and there is a demand for this equipment. Mercury is retrograde May 15; there is an eclipse on May 28 at 5 degrees Sagittarius close to Saturn at 9 degrees Gemini and where Mercury went retrograde at 9 degrees Gemini on May 15.

the United States. The cataclysmic change in the workforce may lead to forming new government-funded work groups, either to send abroad or to work here at home. There are a lot of talented individuals in the United States and this work force will be starving for something to do. Since the transition has thrown many people out of their comfort zone, retraining should be an option that is considered.

As organization mergers continue, more employees will be released and temporary employment agencies may flourish during this time. Manufacturing businesses will cut back as demand and production decline, leaving many in the labor force struggling. Unions may be called upon to increase their assistance to members, and union laws may change so that people are allowed to work in nonunion jobs during this difficult time. Acting as agents for their union members, the union organizations may begin a placement type of service for their members.

People are ready to spend but won't because taxes are due in April 2002. The government, recognizing this, may transform their hard-line position about on-time payment of taxes, offering alternative payment plans or monthly payment with historically low rates. A new model for a flat tax structure may briefly appear on the scene, but it doesn't take hold yet, due to more immediate difficulties that must be addressed, such as the increasing losses in the travel industry. Serious talks about large airline mergers may surface.

Increased cash flow may result from increased exports. Machinery, iron, steel, equipment, military machines, and military trainers are all highlighted as part of this export of product, manufactured goods, and trainers.

Think twice before investing during this quarter. What you may think of as a good investment—one that shows growth or a return to its original price range—may only be reflecting a temporary bump. It is very important to research investments because this quarter brings some incredible bargains. A possible consolidation in mid-May may find our markets overrun by mergers and buyouts between companies. During the second half of May there are several planetary patterns that indicate this final housecleaning in the markets before the mid-summer quarter when things begin to come back to former levels.

Summer Quarter: *June 21, 2002, 9:24 A.M. EDT*[9]

There are a lot of indicators of recovery. June, however, shows a very slow start. Successful results are seen as summer comes to an end and we move into fall, offering new investment possibilities, particularly in the medical, biotech, biochemical, hospitalization, hospital services, medical services, and drug and alcohol rehabilitation arenas. Though oil prices have remained low, they may start creeping up in this quarter. A more drastic price acceleration may occur closer to August 2002.

---

9. *Summer Quarter Astronotes:* Jupiter is close to Mars and Venus in the Twelfth House, indicating strength in hospital, biomedical, and related fields. Astrologically, this seems to be an optimistic quarter. For example, the Mars/Vesta (an asteroid) conjunction usually indicates new investment activity, and this occurs right at the ingress. Mercury and the Sun are conjunct on July 22. Jupiter conjuncts Venus as it enters Leo in early August. And, finally, Mars and the Sun conjunct the chart Ascendant at 14 degrees Leo on August 7, 2002. Expect increased optimism and speculative inclinations of buyers. Jupiter/Mars will be conjunct in late degrees of Cancer on July 5, increasing the spending on housing, food, or antiques.

People are in the mood to start spending during this quarter. Projections are optimistic and investors begin to return to their portfolios to add investments. Even the housing market, with the assistance of low taxes and low mortgage rates, begins to improve. Prices on housing are not at the highs they were in 2000, but they are holding value again, and the next few months may be a good time to invest in real estate or land, while the rates still remain low. In the fall quarter, however, the interest rates look as though they begin to rise and the debt load increases.

The summer quarter may be *the* time to consolidate, re-finance, reposition, and rework our investments to grab onto the best prices in town before the fall quarter begins.

Fall Quarter:
September 23, 2002, 12:55 A.M. EDT[10]

The fall quarter starts out with a bang after the optimism in late July. However, it is important to continue careful spending habits, and follow more traditional investment habits cultivated throughout this very harsh last year. The economy will struggle, not because there aren't jobs, but because of debt that has been incurred in order to sustain ourselves

---

10. *Fall Quarter Astronotes:* There is an eclipse on beginning on November 19, 2002, that signals a tough stretch economically. Venus is retrograde from October 11 to November 21, suggesting caution. Neptune in the Eighth House in Aquarius squaring Venus in the Fifth House suggests fluctuating in oil prices. Jupiter retrogrades on the same day of the eclipse December 4, 2002, in the Second House of earning power, a helpful sign. Saturn, ruling the Seventh House of relations, is in the Twelfth House of this chart, and Mars squares it, indicating that decisions and deals made in late 2001 now come up for re-evaluation.

through the previous year. This is why it is very important to continue on a more conservative investment path. Exercise caution when making purchases and forming legal partnerships, particularly between October 11 and November 21. All contracts require extra care during this period in order to make sure they are workable. Seek out the assistance of an attorney in making sure that all verbiage is correct.

Oil prices that were stable and steady throughout the past year may begin creeping up. The costs of labor and goods remain low, particularly as we move towards the latter part of this quarter.

The strains of this quarter may have something to do with the alliances that were formed during the fight against the terrorist network. It may be time to pay the piper in terms of what we have previously promised.

Meditations on the Future

JONATHAN KEYES

Even as the shock waves from the attack on America sink into our consciousness, we must now prepare for the next inevitable step in what President Bush calls the "war on terrorism." Bush says that this will be a long and protracted affair, that we will "root out evil" and "smoke [terrorists] from their holes." Though many parallels have been made between this attack and the Pearl Harbor attack of 1941, there are stark differences as well. After the attack on Pearl Harbor, America mobilized to fight a distinct enemy, the Axis of Japan, Germany, and Italy. Eventually, America and its allies went on to defeat its enemies and win that war. In this modern attack, the enemy is not so visible. No one has claimed responsibility for the attack, and there are no huge armies that we are fighting against. There is no defined infrastructure to bomb. Our enemy is diffuse and intermingled with civilian populations in many different countries.

In this new war, the United States is up against well-trained, sophisticated terrorists who operate in small, very secret cells. They do not fight in the open with missiles and tanks, but covertly, with bombs and guerrilla tactics. This is a more dangerous type of war in many ways, one similar to the Vietnam conflict. It is difficult to know when victory will be achieved. We also risk a greater escalation of war if we provoke Muslim hatred for our actions. While we have to be careful to eliminate risks to our national security, we also must play a diplomatic role that ensures safety to our country in the future. If we act savagely, we are sure to invoke the wrath of new generations of fanatics, who will be bent on destroying the United States. It is likely that the cost to support and train the hijackers was low, making terrorism is cheap and easy to accomplish. On the other hand, eliminating the global threat of terrorism will be difficult and costly.

What's Ahead for President Bush?

To understand the current situation and where this new war may be headed, it is helpful to examine the charts of the current leaders. One of the most important charts to look at is the chart of President George W. Bush. I discussed some points about Bush's birth chart in the section "Attack on America." Here, I will look at how current astrological transits are interacting with and affecting his birth chart.

During this intense time, Bush has several transits that are important to look at. Transits signify current planetary alignments that can reflect strong transformations in day-to-day activities. The planet Neptune[1] is making a strong aspect to Bush's birth chart. Astrologically, Neptune is associated with spirituality and mysticism, as well as confusion and deception. On a material level, Neptune is associated with oil and with nerve gas weapons. Transits of Neptune can create foggy weather; they can also have the effect of making situations and thinking cloudy or unclear.

In Bush's case, the transit of Neptune first affected him in February of this year,[2] when there was great question about his presidency and whether he was competent to lead a divided nation. Certainly, there were many people who opposed Bush and who wanted to increase doubt about his right to the office.

As the Neptune transit continued to intensify,[3] the attack on September 11 rallied Congress and the nation around him, and questions concerning the legitimacy of his presidency disappeared. Bush has gone on the offensive to say that this country is "strong" and ready for a war against terrorism. However, this war is filled with many pitfalls and confusing issues. The terrorist threat is diffuse and hard to pin down. Choosing who and what to attack will prove to be very difficult. The war may expand to other

---

1. Neptune is conjunct Bush's Descendant. This conjunction is exact on December 21, 2001.

2. Neptune crossed the Descendant degree for the first time on February 17, 2001. Astrologically, the Descendant is associated with one's friends as well as one's enemies.

3. Because of apparent retrograde motion of the planets, relative to the Earth, planets may occupy the same point more than once in a short time period. Neptune first contacted Bush's Descendant on February 17, 2001, the on August 10, 2001, and it will contact for a third time December 12, 2001.

Arab countries, and there is a lack of clarity on how it will proceed.[4]

In the spring of 2002, there are likely to be a series of confusing and cloudy issues concerning the ongoing war. Bush may have difficulty communicating his strategy and coming to clear decisions with his cabinet. He may also have difficulty in his thinking process about the war, and he may have a hard time conveying information to the American public. Furthermore, factors out of his control—oil supplies, Saddam Hussein, or other terrorist actions, such as chemical or biological warfare—may cause a deepening of the conflict at this time.[5]

Along with this Neptune transit, Bush is also experiencing other planetary alignments.[6] The planet Mars is being contacted in Bush's chart and will continue to be affected for the duration of his four-year term as president. Mars relates to one's capacity to fight, and in Bush's case, to wage war. With Mars so prominently affected, it is likely that this presidency will be dominated by the theme of war. March of 2002 may also be a time of a setback for Bush, and possibly for American forces abroad. Bush has to be careful about how he approaches the conflict and beware of escalating his battle plans at that time.[7]

---

4. These are all symbolized by Neptune crossing near Bush's Descendant and opposing his Ascendant.

5. Neptune opposes Mercury on March 8, 2002, and then Pluto on April 5, 2002.

6. Secondary progressed Mars is squaring his natal Sun.

7. Along with the progressions and the Neptune transit, transiting Saturn will be squaring his natal Mars.

Dick Cheney[8]

Though George Bush's chart shows significant astrological activity during this time, the vice president, Dick Cheney, has an equal amount of trying and difficult contacts. Transiting Neptune will conjunct his Sun (associated with one's overall radiance, vigor, and vitality, as well as one's heart[9]). This will be a time when Cheney's essential health and well-being may be threatened. He may have increasing problems with his heart, something that has been an ongoing concern to him. He will also be going through a confusing and uncertain time in which old ways of doing things will dissolve. This may mean that his role in the conflict will become increasingly muddied and he may have a destabilizing effect on the decision making process. As a long-time player in the oil world, his interest in the Middle East oil regions may be too influential in his decision making process. One possibility is that he will advocate escalation of the conflict in order to protect United States economic and oil interests.

Not only is there an increasing involvement of Neptune on Cheney's chart next spring, but Pluto will make contact with his Mars.[10] Pluto, as previously mentioned, is associated with powerful and intense transformations. There is speculation that the White House was a terrorist target,

---

8. Astrological chart information compiled from Lois Rodden's Astro-DataBank at www.astrodatabank.com/NM/CheneyDickDB.htm.

9. Neptune was within one degree of an exact conjunction on March 7, 2001, and will be exact on April 18, 2002.

10. Transiting Pluto will be conjoining his natal Mars in March of 2002. The exact aspect is not completed because Pluto retrogrades.

thereby making Cheney a target of assassination. He was in the White House during the attacks, and was immediately taken to a secure bunker beneath the building. Due to the ongoing transits, Cheney should be careful of a threat against his life, either from terrorists, or as a result of his general health. This threat continues until October 2003.

Osama bin Laden

As a key figure in this war, Osama bin Laden will play an essential role in the conflict to come. Already, he has called on Muslims throughout the world to take up arms against America in a holy war.[11] We do not have an exact birth date for bin Laden, which makes it impossible to draw any specific conclusions about transits to his birth chart. More than likely, however, this is just as confusing a time for him as it is for the rest of us. He has to eat, breathe, and sleep with every thought directed towards possible capture or elimination by U.S. forces. Bin Laden is likely blinded by his dogmatic and tyrannical arrogance, and may feel himself invincible. His stature among Muslims may become even greater if he is killed, though, for then he will likely be seen as a martyr by those willing to continue on with greater fervor for the cause. Neptune is associated with the process of surrender to the divine and to martyrdom, concepts that are strongly forwarded by bin Laden.

---

11. Bernard Lewis, "Muslim Militants Reveal Different View of the World," (*Oregonian: Foreign Affairs*, September 16, 2001), A14. Bin Laden lays out his case for a holy war in a set of pronouncements.

It is interesting to note that President Bush and Vice President Cheney are both experiencing a strong transit of Neptune. This convergence of transits shows that energies associated with Neptune will play a key role in this entire war. In essence, the war is defined as unclear about its eventual aims (to eliminate terrorism), difficult in its process (Afghanistan has been a quagmire for British and Soviet armies), and ultimately focused of issues surrounding oil and the fuel economy.

Saddam Hussein

Though part of the battle may be won with bin Laden's demise, it is likely that new information or action will implicate Saddam Hussein[12] in this war on terrorism. Hussein has played a large role in Middle East politics since before the Gulf War in 1991. Because George Bush Sr. decided not to continue the attack on Iraq until Baghdad was captured and Hussein was imprisoned or eliminated, Hussein has played the role of partial victor over the United States, biding his time to inflict misery on this country once again. After the war, the United States government placed an embargo on Iraq that led to many thousands of civilian deaths due to inadequate food and water. Along with the destructive assault on Iraq during the war, most fundamentalist Muslims, including bin Laden, were outraged by the embargo and feel that a military response is necessary.

---

12. This chart data is taken from Lois Rodden's AstroDataBank at www. astrodatabank.com/NMHusseinSaddam.htm.

Hussein has regularly trained and given money to terrorist organizations bent on destroying America. He has stockpiled chemical weapons, such as nerve gas and, possibly, anthrax. To understand Hussein's role in this conflict, it is important to look at his chart. Hussein's chart shows him to be a volatile and intense man who can be erratic and tempestuous in his ways.[13]

Like George W. Bush and Dick Cheney, Hussein has important points in his chart that will be affected by the current Neptune transit. This transit will be at the peak of its strength between January and April 2002.[14]

Numerous factors seem to be pointing toward the next few months as key to a change in the fabric of the war. I suggest that if bin Laden is killed during this conflict, a greater conflict will emerge that involves Iraq. It is likely that President Bush will feel it necessary to go into Iraq to depose Hussein. This may come as a pre-emptive strike against future violence, because of Iraqi aggression, due to implications that Iraq was involved in the attack on September 11. Because Neptune is associated with oil and chemical/biological weapons, the transit of Neptune shows the possibility that oil or chemical weapons could be involved in this situation. Hussein previously bombed oil fields and could sponsor biological or nerve gas attacks.

Again, the situation will be unclear and confusing. There is difficulty in demarcating strict starting and stopping

---

13. Sun conjoined Uranus along with a Moon/Mars conjunction in Sagittarius.

14. Neptune is now making a square to his Sun/Uranus conjunction.

points to this conflict. Do we just eliminate Hussein or do we work to create a new Iraqi government? Do we station troops in Iraq or do we make a surgical strike to eliminate Hussein? Many of these questions are difficult to answer. Though this series of transits show the possibility of numerous damaging manifestations, it should be noted that there is an astrological aphorism that "Neptune promises much but delivers little." It is possible that events could take a less menacing turn and that less dramatic events could unfold. It is important, however, to be prepared for all eventualities.

Israel

There is no question that Israel plays a pivotal role in this conflict. Israel itself has seen a Neptune transit.[15] Israel needs to act carefully in this deepening conflict and choose ways to reduce conflict and enmity. Choosing to sit down with organizations such as the PLO and their leader Yasser Arafat and discuss ways of compromise can go a long way toward diffusing tensions. Creating a peace plan that will withstand the effects of a few militant terrorist bombings is key to Israel's future success. It is also the key to helping reduce the conflict that the United States is involved in on a larger scale.

---

15. Interestingly, Israel's Moon (the source of its emotional strength) is located only three degrees away from bin Laden's Sun and George Bush's Ascendant at 7 degrees Leo.

16. Uranus will be making a square to the Sun exact on January 24, 2002. It then goes on to oppose natal Mars on April 28, 2002.

Uranus will be active in the chart of Israel from January to May of 2002.[16] In this case, the nation of Israel is about to undergo a serious and sudden change, which could precipitate other events in April or May. Israeli retaliation in these situations may alienate United States support. The United States has been strongly pressuring Israel to make peace in the occupied territories so as to not broaden the conflict.

Conclusion

As we enter this time of instability and confusion, it is important to remember that we are not ruled by the planets. We have the free will to decide to work with these times. Though events may happen out of our control such as terrorism, we can choose how we want to respond to ensure the safety of citizens as well as protecting the world from a future rise in violence. As the United States government makes choices for our future, we should encourage them to act wisely and prudently. In confusing times, it is essential not to increase the confusion. In unpredictable times, it is essential not to increase the volatility.

One of the things that the United States government and citizens can do is to gain a deeper understanding and clarity about the history and background of all the Middle Eastern nations involved. We can become more wise and knowing about how United States foreign policy has impacted those countries and we can seek to choose better ways of acting in the future. We can seek to create a dialogue with Muslim leaders and clerics to promote religious tolerance and understanding and bridge the gap of ignorance. By reaching out through dialogue, we can help to dispel some of the feelings of animosity that lie bare in Arab countries. By asking questions and seeking to understand, we can help to dissuade further acts of violence.

The Saturn/Pluto relationship in the sky right now has much to do with the transformation of the soul of America. Will we choose to move towards further isolation, fostering fear, and further violence, or will we choose to see the root causes of suffering and our role in this suffering? Will we choose to bring to justice only the perpetrators of these terrorist acts, or will we let our anger hurt the lives of millions of innocent civilians? These are questions that we will answer over time. But it is clear that the United States has large decisions to make in this process. Let us hope that they are wise decisions and lead to greater peace and understanding instead of greater hatred and violence.

Recommended Reading

Next: The Future Just Happened by Michael Lewis (WW Norton & Co.: 2001).

101 Things You Can Do for Our Children's Future by Richard Louv (Anchor: 1994).

Leadership in a Time of Terror

Kris Brandt Riske

Most agree the United States is the world's most pow-erful nation and the leader in global politics and economics. Although a young nation, America has long held its coveted position in the world because its high form of democracy has served the causes of national freedom, individual rights, and economic prosperity.

Americans expect the leaders of this great country to be strong in times of crisis, demanding that they meet an un-written standard of leadership. Whether they vote or not, citizens expect their elected and appointed officials to rise to the occasion. Some of our leaders have met or exceeded America's challenges and, of course, others have failed. Presidents, cabinet members, members of Congress, sena-tors, other government officials, and military officers are long remembered for both their heroics and their failures. They are most remembered for their actions in times of crisis—war, economic peril, and homeland disasters. No one, however, has faced a crisis of the magnitude that befell the United States on September 11, 2001. On that day, America's leaders found themselves on the defensive in a war against an unknown enemy—terrorists.

America's top leaders—President George W. Bush, Vice President Dick Cheney, Secretary of State Colin Powell, and Secretary of Defense Donald Rumsfeld—became four of the most important men on the face of the Earth. They are the authors of the first chapters in the world's new future. Many say the American way of life—that adventuresome, freedom-loving mindset that welcomed immigrants from every nation—is forever changed. That remains to be seen. But whatever transpires, these leaders who have been chosen to fight America's war on terrorism, are the ancestors of future immigrants and future Americans.

Leadership: What Is It?

Is it possible to see a leader on a resumé? Can we hear leadership in campaign speeches? Do people have an accurate sense for who is a leader and who is not? Does a candidate's charisma win an election? Is there any rhyme or reason to why a few individuals rise to the most powerful positions in the world? What qualities separate leaders from followers? Are leaders born that way, or are they the products of their times? Is leadership real or manufactured? Finally, can astrology, behavioral science, or public observation answer these questions about leadership?

It is commonly agreed upon that leadership encompasses vision, empowerment, communication, and trust. Leadership is recognizable in action; and you know a leader when you see one. Warren Bennis, an advisor to four American presidents, leadership guru, and author, says, "The essence of leadership is still character. The essence of character is integrity, passion, curiosity, daring, and a guiding vision, without which a leader doesn't know what he wants to do or where he wants to go." He further defines leaders as people who "must be articulate, energetic, and empowering. They must be willing to inspire a collaborative approach that lets them tap into the endless source of ideas, innovation, know-how, and knowledge of the people they lead."[1]

Although the consensus among professionals in the field is that leaders are made, not born, they also concede that great leaders are a rarity. Some people certainly have a knack or talent for leadership. Their natural abilities lend themselves more readily, however, to the lessons of trial-and-error, and experimentation.

What about the question: Can astrology provide clues and insight into leaders themselves? Yes. Astrology's symbolic language makes it possible to quantify leadership traits through planets, signs, and house placement. For example, pragmatic vision could be described by the planets Saturn, Neptune, and Uranus; communication via the planet Mercury and the zodiacal sign Gemini; trust, including accountability, would be attributed to Jupiter and Saturn; and relationship skills to Venus and the Seventh House of the horoscope. Leadership skills, in general, are attributed to the

---

1. Jim Murray, "Thoughts on Leadership from Warren Bennis," August 1997. Available online at www.leader-values.com.

fire signs (Aries, Leo, Sagittarius), the Sun and Mars. Pluto, associated with power, is often prominent in the horoscopes of people in such positions.

The late astrologer Margaret Hone cited factors that strengthened the influence of certain planets. "The strength of Angularity is better expressed by saying that planets are undoubtedly strong when they are close to one of the angles, especially the Ascendant and Midheaven . . ."[2] Astrologers would expect leaders to have a strong Sun, Moon, Mars, or Pluto, for example, conjunct the Ascendant or Midheaven.[3]

The extensive research conducted by Michel Gauquelin also revealed factors prominent in the horoscopes of executives, military leaders, and politicians, among others. Politicians were found to have the Moon and Jupiter prominently placed near an angle in their charts; executives and military personnel have a high frequency of Mars and Jupiter near an angle.[4]

Overall, however—and to speak to misconceptions about astrology and how it might influence world leaders in the aftermath of September 11—planetary influence is not an exact one. Astrology illuminates potentials, tendencies, talents, trends, traits, conflicts, and a host of other pos-

---

2. Margaret Hone, *The Modern Text-Book of Astrology* (Fowler, 1995), 91.

3. See Robert Hand, "Putting Events on the World Map," in this book for more discussion about the importance of planets near the Angles of a chart.

4. Michel Gauquelin, *Planetary Heredity*. Reprinted in the United States by ACS Publications, 1988, 12.

sibilities and choices according to a person's birth chart. But that's only half the story. Environmental, circumstantial, and other nonastrological situations, coupled with astrological conditions, determine actions and their resultant outcomes. A hypothetical example would be a young man with a talent for artistic painting. Planetary and environmental influences *could* steer such a man in opposite directions. He could become a respected artist with his works in the finest galleries, or he could become an inmate in a county jail because he painted gang graffiti on a public building.

Leadership is all about the choices made among personalities who act and react according to a combination of widely varying degrees of nonastrological and astrological influences.

Leadership Responds to Public's Needs

Immediately after the events of September 11, Americans looked to governmental leaders for truthful information. We wanted as clear a vision as possible of the future, based on the goals, objectives, strategies, and actions of our leaders' response to the terrorist attacks. We wanted our leaders to be sensitive to our personal needs and our profound sense of grief. We wanted to trust our leaders to be accountable and reliable. When our expectations were met, American's saw its leaders standing tall, and believed that actions were being taken in the best interests of the country and our people—the public's fears were calmed.

President George W. Bush immediately responded to all American's need to know that we had a leader by speaking briefly to reporters within an hour after the first plane sliced into the World Trade Center and exploded. "This is a difficult time for America," the president said. He ordered a massive investigation and promised to "hunt down the folks who committed this act."

Aboard Air Force One en route to Offutt Air Force Base in Omaha, Nebraska, Bush and his aides decided they didn't want to wait until they reached the base to make another public statement. Sensitive to the people's need for reassurance, the president ordered the plane to stop at Barksdale Air Force Base in Louisiana, where he spoke briefly. Later in the day, he spoke from a protective bunker near Omaha.

As a result of these and subsequent actions, Bush received a public approval rating of 92 percent, the highest ever for a president. He exemplified true leadership by putting the needs of his constituents—the American public—first, and he clearly rose to the occasion, living up to the promise seen in his horoscope, which is, in several respects, an unlikely one for a president.[5] His indomitable inner strength and love of country came to the fore on September 11, 2001. The country responded by placing its trust in the president to handle the calamity. Great leaders,

---

5. Bush has a Twelfth House Sun, usually an indication of someone who prefers to stay out of the limelight. He also has no planets in the Tenth House of reputation and public prominence. His outgoing Leo Ascendant helps to overcome the Twelfth House Cancer Sun, and Venus trine the Midheaven adds to his public persona and popularity. The Twelfth House Sun and Saturn are indicative of inner strength and dependability.

says author Warren Bennis, are trusted because they are seen as sincere. "There is no such thing as instant trust," Bennis said. "Trust has to be earned. A leader can't be phony because people can easily detect phoniness. One of the ways we generate and sustain trust is by caring about the fate of others, by being on their side."

President George W. Bush

The son of former President George H. W. Bush, George W. Bush grew up in Texas, earned a bachelor's degree from Yale and an MBA from Harvard. He served the military as a pilot in the Texas Air National Guard before beginning a career in the oil and gas business. He was a part owner of the Texas Rangers baseball team, and Texas elected him its governor. In the most closely contested and divisive election in American history, George W. Bush was elected president of the United States and took office January 20, 2001.

Self-conscious and tense at times, President Bush, nevertheless, has an overall enthusiastic, energetic, confident nature that leans toward the cautious and conservative. His high, unshakeable principles and intense sense of fair play contribute to his abilities as a diplomat and peacemaker. Bush dislikes discord, but, in a crisis, his inner strength and love of country dominate situations and resultant decisions. He is a staunch defender of America. The president is loyal and sentimental, efficient and fastidious, strong yet sensitive, compassionate and caring.

He has good instincts regarding his relationship with the public, Congress, and members of his administration. He understands the value of teamwork and has a talent for appointing or assigning the right people for the right jobs. Responsibilities weigh heavily on him—in part because of his strong ethics—but he rises to the occasion regardless of the weight of the undertaking.

It is Bush's mind that is his greatest asset. He is a creative and exceptionally balanced thinker—idealistic, yet practical and intuitive. This combination produces strong opinions. Intense and shrewd, he can develop deep insight into any situation and excels at strategic planning, particularly large clandestine operations. Extremely tight-lipped—almost secretive—he reveals only what he wants to reveal. Intelligent and generally happy with his decisions, he uses an analytical, commonsense approach to problems.[6]

As a speaker, Bush goes directly to the point and is a better communicator when using a prepared speech than when talking off the cuff. He occasionally fails to say what he means, but such was not the case when he addressed a joint session of Congress in a nationally televised speech September 20, 2001. There he succinctly laid out the mission for the country and its allies.

"Our nation—this generation—will lift a dark threat of violence from our people and our future," the president said. "We will rally the world to this effort by our efforts

---

6. Mercury conjunct Pluto conjunct the Leo Ascendant, an aspect that signals unwavering power, drive, determination, and a razor-sharp mind. A Third House Neptune adds vision and optimism, as does a Moon/Jupiter conjunction in the same house trine Uranus. On its own, Pluto conjunct the Ascendant is an aspect that denotes strength and control in crisis situations.

and by our courage. We will not tire, we will not falter, and we will not fail."

In those few sentences, Bush displayed leadership through vision,[7] communication, trust, and empowerment. He delivered a message that America's war on terrorism is not his alone—it is one that includes America speaking to the world, saying that the world cannot let what happened to America happen to it.

Warren Bennis says leadership is "the capacity to create a compelling vision and translate it into action and sustain it. Successful leaders have a vision that other people believe in and treat as their own."

Vice President Richard Cheney

Vice President Dick Cheney, a seasoned conservative politician and staunch supporter of a stronger national defense, has long ties to the Bush family. He served as secretary of defense under former President Bush during the Gulf War. Cheney also represented Wyoming in the U.S. House of Representatives and was former President Gerald R. Ford's chief of staff.

Eminently capable and a master organizer, the *New York Times* reported he was "widely credited with taking an administration [Ford's] in disarray and bringing it under control. Cheney's strong drive and work ethic were major influences in shaping up Ford's White House. He demands

---

7. In an April 20–22, 2001, CNN/*USA Today*/Gallup Poll, 74 percent of Americans said Bush has a vision for his presidency.

excellence from both his self and from others, yet likes to set his own rules and parameters.[8]

Cheney is a study in contrasts. His relentless determination is masked by a vivacious, ultracharming, magnetic persona. He draws a crowd and senses what people want, the result of highly developed psychic/intuitive powers, but at the same time, he can be as critical and cold as he is charismatic, warm, and outgoing. He easily adapts to circumstances—an asset to any politician. He is very much a "people person," going that extra mile to be helpful.[9]

A team player, Cheney nevertheless has an independent streak and, like President Bush, he can let his overly optimistic attitude get carried away. Again, like the president he answers to, Cheney does not shy away from monumental tasks. Future oriented and attuned to the final outcome, he too grasps the concept of vision. Cheney is pragmatic and possesses the common sense that is invaluable in translating vision into goals, objectives, strategies, and tactics.[10]

---

8. Dick Cheney's Ascendant is Virgo, the sign of the fastidious workaholic and one that excels at administration, organization, detail, and analysis. His two Sixth House planets (Sun and Mercury) reinforce the Virgo emphasis. He also has a Sun/Pluto/Jupiter/Saturn T-square that gives him independence, a drive for power and control, and often indicates one who easily intimidates and is demanding. A "take charge" aspect, it is invaluable in times of crisis.

9. Cheney's Venus/Mercury/Neptune grand trine is extremely charismatic, and his sensitive, compassionate Pisces Moon in the Seventh House of relationships add to his easy (and intuitive) way with people. A Moon/Neptune/Mars T-square is an asset in putting vision into action. These configurations and his Sun/Pluto opposition suggest insight and psychic ability.

10. Cheney's Sun and Mercury in the future-oriented sign of Aquarius are sensitive to the final outcome, as is Bush's Jupiter/Uranus trine.

Cheney can display a stubborn determination that is married to his ideas, ideals, and beliefs. He is also innovative and imaginative; he's an individual who comes up with nonconformist ideas that are the missing-link solutions to otherwise puzzling dilemmas. He recognizes, seizes, and capitalizes on opportunities with a sense of adventure and a courageous "go for it" attitude.[11]

Ironically, in June 2001, Bush assigned Cheney the task of developing a task force to study the threat of domestic terrorism, including whether the Federal Emergency Management Agency (FEMA) or another government agency should coordinate the response to threats. On September 11, 2001, terrorism on homeland soil became reality, and Cheney, Bush, Secretary of Defense Donald Rumsfeld, and Secretary of State Colin Powell responded.

Secretary of State Colin L. Powell

Secretary of State Colin Powell's cool, calm demeanor inspires people's confidence in him. It's a subtle detachment that exudes confidence. (All that he has to do is walk into a room.) Powell is a skilled proponent for empowering those around him, a philosophy and talent that has impressed and pleased State Department employees.

Many State Department employees say that morale has increased dramatically under Powell. "Since he took over, there is a feeling that the leadership is open to the views and expertise of its staff, and is no longer a closed group of

---

11. Cheney has six planets in fixed signs, including Mercury in Aquarius, sign of the innovator. His Mars in Sagittarius signifies courage, action, and enthusiasm.

people." The biggest boost to morale has been Powell's own personality and style, especially his pledge to rely on the rank-and-file experts in the department for higher-profile roles, rather than simply the anonymous drafting of papers that bigwigs deliver at hearings and conferences.[12]

This secretary of state clearly understands leadership principles—the need for strong relationships and communication. Seven of the thirteen "Powell Rules" (his personal philosophy) are: "It can be done," "Share credit," "Remain calm," "Be kind," "Have a vision," "Be demanding," and "Perpetual optimism is a force multiplier." That he is a respected leader is no surprise because, as one leadership expert cites, the military is known as one of the finest leadership training programs in existence.

Powell excelled in the Army Reserve Officer Training Corps (ROTC) program in college, eventually rising to the rank of four-star general before his retirement from the military in 1993. A two-tour veteran of Vietnam, he received numerous medals and citations, including the Purple Heart, Bronze Star, and Congressional Gold Medal. He served as national security adviser under former President Ronald Reagan. As chairman of the Joint Chiefs of Staff under President Bush's father, he was instrumental in the execution of Desert Storm during the Gulf War. He, Bush, and Cheney have since been criticized for not finishing that war by either eliminating or deposing Saddam Hussein of Iraq. Powell continued his Joint Chiefs chairmanship under

---

12. Ben Barber, "The Colon Powell Difference," May 19, 2001. Available online at www.salon.com.

President Bill Clinton. At times, he has been mentioned as a possible presidential candidate.

Fearless, action-oriented, courageous, and dynamic, Colin Powell is steady, idealistic, reliable, and conservative, with an inner strength of will and determination. He rarely, if ever, backs down from his objective. High principles and integrity form his belief system, credos that distinctly separate right from wrong.[13]

Powell maintains objectivity and thus can be perceived as detached. Often referred to as charismatic, he knows the value of teamwork, the importance of sharing the load. A pleasant voice adds to his strong communication skills, which feature tact and persuasion. An excellent debater, his mind is quick and intelligent, as well as intense and secretive.[14]

---

13. Powell's strong Pluto conjunct the Ascendant opposes Jupiter and trines Saturn. Jupiter also sextiles Saturn in mutual reception (Capricorn, Pisces) and thus functions much like a conjunction. Powell has an iron will, the "iron fist in a velvet glove," a sense for when to push forward and when to maintain the status quo. The Saturn/Pluto trine is possibly the single most dynamic aspect that promises a powerful position in life. His Aries Sun and Mercury, and his Sagittarius Mars are ideal for a military officer. He acts without hesitation.

14. Mercury in Aries conjunct Venus in Taurus gives him the best of both signs, the ability to make quick, practical decisions and present them diplomatically to generate support. Mercury square Pluto is secretive and intense; he speaks with conviction. An Aquarius Moon in the Seventh House of relationships is excellent for teamwork and objectivity.

With his military background and outstanding people skills, Powell is well suited to the position of secretary of state, the office responsible for America's diplomatic relations with foreign countries. He wrote, "War should be the politics of last resort," and he has said, "When the United States goes to war, it should be for a clear purpose, and the outcome should be overwhelming victory."[15] His philosophy rings loudly in decisions made in America's war on terrorism.

Secretary of Defense Donald Rumsfeld

Secretary of Defense Donald Rumsfeld left a meeting on missile defense when word came of the attacks on the World Trade Center in New York City. According to Congressman Christopher Cox, Rumsfeld said, "Let me tell ya, I've been around the block a few times. There will be another event." (And he repeated the statement for emphasis.) "And within minutes of saying that, his words proved tragically prophetic," said Cox. Rumsfeld was in his office on the opposite side of the Pentagon building in Arlington, Virginia, when American Airlines Flight 77 crashed into the building.[16]

A Navy veteran and four-term congressman in the 1960s, Donald Rumsfeld served his first stint as secretary of defense in the Ford administration, where, previously, he

---

15. Seven Mufson, "Reluctant Warrior Is Political Veteran," *Washington Post*, December 16, 2000.
16. "Pentagon Attack Came Minutes After Rumsfeld Predicted," Associated Press, online at www.foxnews.com, September 11, 2001.

was Ford's chief of staff and Dick Cheney's boss. Like Bush and Cheney, he has been a corporate executive.

As secretary of defense, Rumsfeld is the principle defense policy adviser to the president and supervises the Department of Defense and its policies, one of which is to build a mightier missile defense system for the United States.

Direct, energetic, optimistic, and adventuresome, Rumsfeld has a "can-do" attitude and is, at heart, more a peacemaker and diplomat than a fighter. His loyalty and love of country were the biggest factors in his agreement to serve a second time at the Department of Defense.[17]

A man with strong people skills and the ability to nurture and support others, the secretary also possesses an outstanding mind. Expansive and creative in his thinking, his mind is quick, observant, and perceptive. He excels at strategic planning, thinks big and speaks his mind. His physical energy is put into first gear behind mental tasks, and, other than the president, he has been the primary spokesman for the defense team.[18]

Like the other three members of America's defense team, Rumsfeld has the intense drive, determination, and will that leads to success and are requisite for powerful positions. He has the passionate commitment his position demands, and he is in his element as a commanding force in crisis situations. A team player, Rumsfeld also has an independent

---

17. A Sagittarius Ascendant adds fire to Rumsfeld's three Cancer (love of country) planets—Sun, Venus, and Pluto—in the Seventh House of relationships. His Moon is in Libra, the sign of the diplomat.
18. The Cancer planets enhance his people skills. His Mercury/Mars sextile indicates a sharp mind that can handle multiple tasks.

streak, during which he prefers to be in total charge, and to structure the environment to suit himself.[19]

Rumsfeld summed up the administration's approach to the war on terrorism in a September 27, 2001, news briefing: "To characterize the administration's approach as measured, I think, would be correct. It is. We are determined to try to do this right, to put in place the capabilities, the architectures, and the process that will enable us to proceed in an orderly way over a sustained period of time. We're trying to help the world understand what it is this is about, and it's new for them as well. And my impression is that you're right, we're not leaping into this, we're moving into it in a measured way."

His words reflect the overall cautious, conservative approach of the Bush administration, plus attention to strategy to maximize the chance of a favorable outcome. What he says also indicates the visioning involved in the process, the clearly defined goals and objectives, as well as a high regard for communication, and trust to empower people and seek their support.

"This war will not be waged by a grand alliance united for the single purpose of defeating an axis of hostile powers," Rumsfeld wrote in a *New York Times* piece. He said different countries that are supporting the United States in its war against terrorism would each have different roles in such a coalition. "In this war, the mission will define the

---

19. Rumsfeld's Seventh House Sun/Pluto conjunction in Cancer gives him the ability to take charge of a situation but still be sensitive to other people. Both planets square Uranus, a configuration that upon occasion can hamper teamwork. A Jupiter/Uranus trine favors group efforts and is helpful and lucky in such endeavors.

coalition—not the other way around." He continued, "The public may see some dramatic military engagements that produce no apparent victory, or may be unaware of other actions that lead to major victories. But if this is a different kind of war," Rumsfeld concluded, "one thing is unchanged: America remains indomitable."

Rumsfeld's message is a collective one that undoubtedly represents the thinking of the Bush-Cheney-Powell-Rumsfeld team. Each of these men contributes to the process, bringing experience, knowledge, individual strengths, as well as weaknesses to the table.

The four men share some common characteristics, chief among them strength, drive, and determination—the ability to take charge of a situation and do their best to resolve it. In their presence, one would surely sense their power, authority, and influence, which are displayed more openly by some members of this team. All are action oriented, loyal, highly principled, but pragmatic.

These men differ somewhat in their modus operandi. All are adaptable to changing conditions—able to switch gears to a new approach when necessary. Cheney and Powell are action oriented in the purest sense. Bush's actions take on a more practical, analytical flavor; and Rumsfeld is the best at covering all the bases, keeping his finger on all areas of activity simultaneously.[20]

---

20. Powell and Cheney have Mars in Sagittarius, Bush has Mars in Virgo, and Rumsfeld has Mars in Gemini. British Prime Minister Tony Blair has Mars in Gemini, and Russian President Vladimir Putin has Mars in Sagittarius. Each is a mutable sign, which suggests a leader's need to be adaptable, to "go with the flow" with changing conditions.

The communication styles of Powell, Rumsfeld, and Bush are more similar, with Powell's being the most direct. All tend to approach things intellectually, having mastered the art of maintaining distance and objectivity while establishing strong connections with people, either in person or through the news media. They effectively balance care and concern, compassion and sensitivity, without letting those personal qualities and emotions heavily influence their decisions and actions.[21]

Bush is well suited for his role as commander in chief of America's war on terrorism. A deep thinker and superb strategist, he is the most likely to have created the basic plan to fight the war at home and on foreign soil. He has the vision and knows how to achieve it. Rumsfeld, second only to Bush as a strategist, is sensitive to how the war will be perceived by American citizens and the people of the world. He sees the need to garner their support to build a grassroots movement; then he will easily take command of implementing the plan.

Cheney adds innovation, imagination, and intuition and, as a master organizer, sizes up the plan from a logistical perspective. He also stresses the importance of communicating the plan to the American people and senses how best to do that. Powell, the most well-rounded leader of the four, views the situation globally, commands the most stature, and helps the others come to consensus by balanc-

---

21. The air element signifies objectivity; the water element governs sensitivity. All four men have a balance of elements, including earth and fire.

ing knowledge from three fronts—his background as a military officer, as a diplomat, and his experience in politics.

As president and vice president, Bush and Cheney are well matched. Bush prefers being behind the scenes, while Cheney is more of an out-front public person and openly enthusiastic. Bush is the thinker. Cheney takes the president's thoughts and puts them into action, polishing it all with creativity and philosophy. Powell is the most public of the four, representing stability, confidence, and trust. Rumsfeld combines diplomacy with action.

This American war team works well together in large part because each member's strong points and areas of emphasis are different. What one has the others don't, and vice versa. They complement each other, each bringing individual strengths to the collective whole. And they have enough in common to relate well to each other.

America is fortunate in this time of crisis to have such able leaders in charge of the country's future. The response to terrorism will require leadership of the type this country has never seen; and nonastrological and astrological influences will make that leadership memorable and successful.

Two other world leaders are likely to have a significant role in America's war on terrorism. They are British Prime Minister Tony Blair and Russian President Vladimir Putin.

Tony Blair pledged his and his country's support of America's efforts to end worldwide terrorism. His attendance at Bush's September 20, 2001, speech to Congress and the nation symbolized that commitment. Like his four American counterparts, Blair is highly principled. "Power without principle is barren, but principle without power is futile," the prime minister said.[22]

An attorney, Blair was first elected to the British Parliament in 1983 and began agitating for change in the Labor Party. After a failed attempt in 1987, he successfully unseating Margaret Thatcher; he went on to became prime minister in a May 1997 landslide election.

A man of incredible action and energy, Blair is intelligent, quick-witted, highly competitive, and focused on achievement. He's also practical, conservative, and cautious. His traits in combination give him the ability to plan, focus on his objectives and turn vision into reality.[23]

Determination is Blair's underlying strength. He is an incredibly hard worker; he is intuitive; and he is immensely popular with the public, in part because of his lively and refreshing charisma. At times, he jumps headlong into a situation, relying on luck to carry him through. It usually does.[24] With Blair, it is easy to assume that "what you see is what you get," but there is far more to him than meets the

---

22. Available online at www.abcnews.go.com.
23. Blair is pure energy with Mars conjunct the Ascendant, and Mercury and Venus in Aries. His Sun and Jupiter in Taurus are down-to-earth, and his knack for realistic vision comes from Saturn conjunct Neptune. With Mars in Gemini he is able to balance multiple tasks.
24. Four planets in the Twelfth House indicate strong intuition, and his Tenth House Moon signifies public prominence. Sun sextile Uranus and Moon sextile Venus, along with his Gemini Ascendant, give him charm and wit. Protective and lucky Jupiter is in the Twelfth House conjunct the Ascendant.

eye. His exuberant personality masks sheer determination and exquisite planning for all he does. Extremely self-motivated, he sets high goals and pushes himself to achieve them. He has the power and drive of a world leader.[25]

Russian President Vladimir Putin pledged his country's support to America's war on terrorism, including troops. Russia waged a long and losing battle with Afghanistan in the late twentieth century. Bush and Putin met face-to-face not long before the terrorist attack on America, and both men told the world, in a news conference, that while they had their differences, the meeting had provided an understanding of each man to the other, Bush even saying he understood Putin's "soul."

Putin, an attorney, succeeded Boris Yeltsin as president of Russia in March 2000. A relative unknown, he was a KGB agent for fifteen years before turning to politics and heading the Federal Security Bureau (successor to the KGB). He served as prime minister for a year before becoming president.

A hard worker with incredible drive and energy, it was almost inevitable that Putin would land in a powerful position. Shrewd and secretive, he is intelligent, creative, and has a knack for turning and using situations to his advantage. His powerful, intelligent mind has penetrating insight and is that of a strategist, planner, and implementer. He

---

25. Saturn sextile Pluto, indicative of people in powerful positions, gives him inner strength and determination, as do his four Twelfth House planets.

chooses words for their impact and is bold, courageous, and forceful.[26]

Putin also is charismatic, a man who has the tact, wit, people skills, and persuasiveness to charm nearly anyone. He easily intuits what individuals and the populace need and want, and he attracts people who bring him luck. The lighter side of Putin is fun-loving, but it is impossible to know his true intent at any given moment.[27]

Recommended Reading

On Becoming a Leader by Warren Bennis (Warren Bennis Inc.: 1994).

Robert E. Lee on Leadership: Executive Lessons on Character by H. W. Crocker III (Prima Publishing: 2000).

---

26. Putin has a Scorpio Ascendant and Pluto conjunct the Midheaven, the most powerful location for that planet, which also is in positive aspect with Mercury, Mars, Saturn, Neptune, and Pluto. His horoscope is ideal for a KGB agent/spy and an extremely powerful world leader who is far better as a friend than an enemy. Like Powell and Cheney, Putin has Mars in Sagittarius.

27. Putin has the Sun and Mercury in Libra and a Gemini Moon. His Seventh House Jupiter indicates luck through other people. Three planets in the Twelfth House show intuition, as does his Scorpio Ascendant.

Where Do We Go from Here?

ROBERT HAND

A s I am writing these words on October 7, 2001, the counter-attack by the United States against the Taliban and Osama bin Laden has begun. It began at about 8:57 P.M. Afghan time (8 hours 30 minutes ahead of Eastern Daylight Time). At this time the Sun in the zodiac was in exactly the same position as the Mercury and Ascendant of the first plane crash into the North Tower of the World Trade Center. This is also the same degree as the Saturn of the Declaration of Independence. I cannot say that I am surprised by the timing of this counterattack as I expected it to come somewhere in the first seven or eight days of October because of the planetary positions and relationships that are forming on these days.

In the days after the attacks, Jupiter began to move into an important position: the degree of the Sun in the Declaration of Independence chart (13 degrees Cancer and 19 minutes), which also happens to be the same degree as the

Sun in George W. Bush's chart (13 degrees Cancer and 49 minutes). These Jupiter to Sun contacts are significant because it indicates the remarkable transformation that has occurred both to the people of the United States and to the presidency of George W. Bush. The people, instead of trembling in fear, have come together; and George W. Bush, whom many previously regarded as lightweight president, has begun to function quite credibly as a leader, pushing his ratings in the opinion polls to some of the highest levels of any president ever.[1]

Jupiter will continue to be at or near these positions until mid-May 2002. And during the autumn of 2001 Jupiter will never get more than a degree and a half or so away from these Sun positions. Jupiter was regarded by the old astrologers as "the greater benefic," being the opposite of Saturn "the greater malefic," and, while it is true that Jupiter is not always good nor is Saturn always bad, it is very clear that these positions of Jupiter bode well for the president and for the feeling of well-being of the people. This is most desirable because this kind of energy is needed to counteract the more difficult side of the Saturn/Pluto combination.

The Chart of the Beginning of the Counterattack

This chart almost looks as if someone had picked it using astrology. In Kabul and environs, Saturn has just risen and

---

1. Of course, opinion polls are a late-twentieth-century phenomenon. We have none for George Washington.

Pluto is setting. This is the very same Saturn–Pluto opposition that seems to have been the long-range timer for this war. The Moon is just about to come into the same degree as Saturn (Moon at 13 degrees 20 minutes of Gemini, Saturn at 14 degrees 52 minutes Gemini). This has the effect of re-energizing the Saturn/Pluto opposition (two planets opposite each other in the zodiac) and the fact that it is doing a rise/set in Afghanistan clearly indicates that Kabul is a place where the effects of the opposition will be felt most strongly.[2]

The degree that the Sun was in at the start of the counterattack is not only conjunct Saturn in the 1776 United States chart and the Ascendant/Mercury in the World Trade Center crash, but it is also entering into a very powerful combination called a *T-square*. A T-square is a combination in which two planets are opposite each other with a third planet at or close to 90 degrees to both of the other two. Mars is roughly opposite Jupiter and the Sun makes the vertical arm of the *T*.[3] It is a combination that indicates great and abundant energy that is forcefully applied, and of course, Mars is the planet of war. It was this T-square that I thought would time our counterattack and so it has turned out to be.

---

2. Saturn is rising and Pluto is setting. See Robert Hand, "Putting Events on the World Map," in this book for information about the importance of planets rising and setting (angular placements).

3. The Sun is at 14 degrees and 28 minutes of Libra, Jupiter at 14 degrees and 36 minutes of Cancer, and Mars is at 16 degrees and 44 minutes of Capricorn.

So Where Do We Go from Here?

Because of the position of Jupiter in the zodiac at present (also known as the *transiting* Jupiter), we can expect reasonable success in the near future, probably through May of 2002. I am not saying that there will not be more incidents caused by the other side, in fact, given the power of the combinations occurring at the present time, something might happen, or at least be attempted, by the other side very soon. And we do still have the Saturn/Pluto combination, indicating restrictions and difficulties. However, the energies indicated by Jupiter are very favorable for the United States and President Bush for several months.

But, beginning in late March 2002, the planet Uranus begins to cross the position of the Moon in the Declaration chart (July 4, 1776). This crossing-over (*transit*) happens several times until January 2003.[4] During the early part of this transit we will still have Jupiter on the Declaration's Sun, but after that the Uranus transit will be operating by itself. So what does this mean? In the chart of a nation, as we mentioned in the article on the United States chart,[5] the Ascendant indicates the people of the nation. But the Ascendant degree is not the only position that indicates this. So does the Moon. So Uranus, the planet of sudden changes and unexpected events, crossing the Moon of the

---

4. The first contact of Uranus to the Moon is on March 3, 2002. The second is on August 11, 2002, and the third is on January 21, 2003.

5. See Jonathan Keyes, "The United States Chart," and Robert Hand, "The United States' Chart," in this book.

Declaration chart indicates the possibility of the United States public becoming increasingly restless and possibly even turbulent. So even though we have been told that this is going to be a very long war, it is clear that the government should try to make as much progress before May 2002 as possible. It is also clear that it would not be a good idea for the government to become too strong in curbing civil liberties in the pursuit of national security during this time. Of course, what must be done must be done, but there do seem to be those in the Bush administration who might have a little too much enthusiasm for curtailing civil liberties.

Interestingly enough, the last time this transit happened was 1918 and 1919 just at the end of World War I when, in fact, there was considerable curtailing of civil liberties. Toward the end of that period the people became very weary of war. There are, I am happy to say, differences between then and now. The government propaganda machine in World War I was very strident and made no effort to inform the American public. It pandered to every prejudice imaginable and tried to obliterate every reference to things German. Sauerkraut became "Liberty Cabbage" and hamburger became "Salisbury Steak." So far in this conflict the government has seemed quite reasonable and has avoided efforts at overt propaganda. The actions of the terrorists seemed to have provided all the motivation that the people need. Another significant difference is that this time the attack was on American soil. This is no small difference.

The Long-Range Picture

The transit of Pluto over the Ascendant of the Declaration of Independence chart is almost over, assuming that we have the time of the signing correct.[6] It was supposed to have signified a major change in the American people. So it seems to have done. No one can argue that we have not suddenly let go of a great deal of the triviality that beset us in the months prior to the World Trade Center attacks. How many people remember Gary Condit?

But will we learn anything new from our current situation? We might learn by examining how we got into this. It is generally recognized that our seemingly unqualified support for Israel has made us few friends in the Islamic world. And elsewhere in that world we support regimes that are not exactly democratic or responsive to their people such as in Saudi Arabia and Egypt. Not only are these regimes not democratic, they are not even liked by their own people. While none of them are as bad as the Taliban, which seems to be actively involved in persecuting and committing general mayhem on their own people, they do not have much popular support, nor are they efficient, honest, or very effective except at staying in power. Then there are the wonderful things that we have done in the past such as supporting Saddam Hussein against the Iranians in the long Iran-Iraq war, a bloody war that further alienated us from the Iranians and certainly did not win us the love of Saddam Hussein. And there was our enthusiastic support for

---

6. See Robert Hand, "The United States' Chart," in this book.

the "freedom fighters" in Afghanistan against the U.S.S.R. in the 1980s. In the course of this we armed, but not exactly won over, the group that would later become the Taliban. What has that to do with the current situation, astrologically speaking, aside from the obvious historical connections? It is very simple. During the Iran-Iraq and Afghanistan-Soviet wars, Saturn and Pluto were making a different, but no less significant, contact.[7]

Cycles of Planets

The late and very influential astrologer Dane Rudhyar[8] was one of the first astrologers to develop a genuinely clear idea of a cycle in astrology and what it meant. He saw the cycle that two planets make with each other as they move about in the zodiac as being something like the growth cycle of a plant. And he patterned his understanding of these cycles on the Sun/Moon, or lunation cycle, that occurs every month.

We are used to thinking in terms of phases with the Sun and Moon, beginning with the New Moon (when the Sun and Moon are in the same degree of the zodiac). This is a conjunction. Then we have the first quarter Moon, when the Moon is 90 degrees beyond the Sun in the zodiac, followed by the Full Moon, which occurs when the Sun and Moon are exactly opposite in the zodiac (opposition). Then

---

7. The last conjunction of Saturn and Pluto occurred in November 1982, when both the Iran-Iraq and the Aghanistan-Soviet wars were taking place.

8. He was influential for very good reasons. He was one of astrology's few intellectuals in his day. In addition to his work with cycles, he developed the body of material upon which modern astrology, particularly psychological astrology, is based.

at last we have the last quarter Moon, when the Moon is 270 degrees ahead of the Sun (or 90 degrees behind it depending on one's point of view) heading back toward the next New Moon. Rudhyar saw that one could examine all cycles of planets in the same way. The cycle begins when the faster planet is conjunct (in the same degree) as the slower moving planet. Then the faster planet gets to 90 degrees ahead of the slow planet (a square), followed eventually by the opposition, and, finally, the second square.

Here is how he used the image of the growth cycle of a flowering plant. The conjunction is like the germination of a seed. At this point something begins and no one really knows how it is going to turn out. Actions taken at the conjunction point of a cycle will have consequences that will not become obvious for some time. Then as the plant begins to grow, it encounters environmental factors that test its development. There is the wind and rain and the lack or presence of sunlight. In a cycle there comes a point where the viability of whatever began at the conjunction is tested. Changes can be made at this time to improve the outcome because it is becoming gradually clear what it is that is coming to be.

In the cycle, this is symbolized by the first square. Then the plant matures and starts to flower. The complete reality of what began at the conjunction is now clear and not much can be done about that reality. In the cycle, this corresponds to the opposition. But even at this point one has not completely lost the ability to effect change. The opposition marks the beginning of the second phase of the cycle. The plant flowers and sets seed, the foundation of the future consequences of the plant's existence is now in place. Do we let the plant set seed? Do we ensure that the seeds will be planted in places where they will grow properly? This is the function of the second half of the cycle.

At the time of the conjunction in 1982 we were entirely concerned with short-range consequences. We wanted the Afghan people to exhaust the Soviet Union. That strategy worked, and the Soviet Union fell apart. But we abandoned the Afghans after they were no longer useful. In the Iran-Iraq war we somewhat favored the Iraqis and propped up the regime of Saddam Hussein. We thought of him as the lesser of two evils between himself and Iran. This did not work and subsequent history suggests that the Iranians may have been the "lesser evil." It now seems entirely possible that Hussein may be working with Osama bin Laden. And on the very day that I write this, bin Laden has spoken via videotape to the effect that our sanctions against Hussein only hurt the Iraqi people. That is one of the alleged acts of "terrorism" that bin Laden has accused us of.

In 1993 and 1994 the cycle of Saturn and Pluto came to the waxing quarter.[9] This was a time when, astrologically speaking, we could have done something about our earlier mistakes. There is probably not much we could have done with Hussein. It was only a couple of years after the Gulf War and we were still trying to overthrow him with our sanctions, which has certainly not worked. In Afghanistan, the rebels that had defeated the Soviets were still fighting each

---

9. There were three squares: one on March 20, 1993; one on October 9, 1993; and one on January2, 1994.

other. The Taliban had not yet come to power. Maybe we could have looked to see which side would be most beneficial for ourselves and for the Afghans at that point in time, but we did nothing.

So here we are at the opposition. The plant has flowered. Saddam Hussein is still in power and has even succeeded in becoming an object of sympathy in some quarters, and he may have been part of what has just happened here in the United States. And in Afghanistan the "flower" is most certainly the Taliban and it is not a pretty sight!

So what can we do? It is not likely that can ever expect our government to be entirely altruistic. There are too many economic interests both in our country and other countries, to expect much that is not ultimately profitable for those interests. But maybe we can ask that they replace mere self-interest with *enlightened* self-interest. What group of economically interested powers can possibly regard the money saved by not helping Afghanistan get on its feet in the 1980s and 1990s as worth cost of the lives and property in the World Trade Center attacks?

The reason why our president seems to be having little trouble forging a coalition against the Taliban and bin Laden is not only because the acts themselves were unbelievably savage, but because they have also been extremely bad for world trade, even for the Arab oil producers, including Saudi Arabia, bin Laden's home country. The recession that is coming upon us will be very bad for the demand for oil. If all of the economic interests can see that having peoples of the Earth living in misery is not only immoral, but ultimately bad for business, maybe something will be done. And this includes not only Afghanistan, but also Africa and everywhere where chronic poverty is a breeding ground for desperate actions.

The next Saturn/Pluto square will occur in August 2010. We must work until then, and especially at that time, to ensure that the seeds being formed now are the kind of seeds that will produce the best results for the United States and for the rest of the world.

Recommended Reading

Culture Matters: How Values Shape Human Progress edited by Lawrence E. Harrison and Samuel P. Huntingdon (Basic Books: 2001).

The Great Conjunctions

ROBERT HAND

Editor's note: This chapter explores the methods used by medieval astrologers to make forecasts. The methods are remarkably like those used today. Robert Hand uses the same charts as the other authors have used. He includes additional charts as well. Hand explains how Persian and Arab astrology works, and he uses those techniques to enhance our understanding of the entire modern period from about 1700 forward. This chapter does contain astrological terminology.

In medieval Persian and Arabic astrology there was an elaborate and sophisticated method for doing long-range historical predictions. It consisted of examining charts surrounding the coming together into single degrees (conjunctions) of the outer planets—Jupiter and Saturn[1]—along with charts erected for the entry of the Sun into the sign Aries. This event signifies the beginning of spring in the Northern Hemisphere.[2] The best and most complete

---

1. For the Persians, Jupiter and Saturn were the outer planets.
2. The beginning of the sign Aries is defined as the point when spring begins.

description of this method was given by the Persian astrologer Abu Ma'shar (A.D. 787–886) in the book known in Arabic as *The Book of Religions and of Dynasties*, and in Latin translation as *On the Great Conjunctions*.[3] In Part I, Chapter 1, he introduces the conjunctions and the method of using them for describing future events. The following is a summary of his description.

1. According to Abu Ma'shar, every 960 years Jupiter and Saturn come together near the beginning of Aries. This is a *Great Conjunction.*

2. Every 240 years the conjunctions of Jupiter and Saturn move from one element to another. What this means will be described shortly. This is called a *Mutation Conjunction,* which simply means a conjunction that changes.

3. Every thirty years Mars and Saturn come together near the beginning of the sign of Cancer.

4. Every twenty years Jupiter and Saturn come together in the same degree. This was later called a *Least Conjunction.*

5. Each year the Sun enters the signs Aries, Cancer, Libra, and Capricorn at the beginnings of each of the seasons. Abu Ma'shar instructs us to also look

---

3. This has been published in an Arabic edition along with a modern English translation and the medieval Latin translation. See Yamamoto and Burnett, *Abu Ma`sar, On Historical Astrology*, two volumes (Leiden: Brill, 2000).

at the charts of the nearest New or Full Moon before each entry.

6. Between the times in number 5 the Sun enters each
   individual sign. He also would like us to look at the
   New or Full Moon that occurs just before that entry.

Now this group of "conjunctions" is a bit different from
those given by other authors. For example, Al Qabisi (known
in Latin as Alchabitius) gives a slightly different list in his in-
troduction.[4] The first four items in the list are the same, but
item number 4 in Al Qabisi's version would have us only
look at the entry of the Sun into Aries (spring), and item
number 5 consists of charts erected for every New and Full
Moon. Unlike modern astrologers who typically look at all
New and Full Moon charts, ancient astrologers looked at
only New and Full Moons charts just prior to the beginning of the seasons.

What is the second type of conjunction? Why is it that
Jupiter and Saturn conjunctions change every 240 years?
Jupiter/Saturn conjunctions occur in groups such that each
conjunction is a bit less than 120 degrees prior to the previous one in the zodiac. This means, eventually the conjunctions move forward from one sign to the next in the zodiac.
See Figure 16 on page 254.

Signs that are 120 degrees apart are said to be in the
same element (triplicity)—fire, air, earth, or water. So for a
while the conjunctions occur in fire signs, for example, but

---

4. al-Qabisi, *Alcabitii ad magisterium astrorum Isagoge* (Paris: 1521), 20
   recto.

gradually move forward into the next element (in this example, the earth element), after which the conjunctions will move into air signs, and so forth. See Figure 16 on page 254. When the conjunctions move from one element to another, that is the *mutation conjunction* referred to above. When this happens astrologers are supposed to erect a chart for the beginning of the nearest previous spring. That chart is supposed to reflect the astrological indicators for the next 240 years.

From the viewpoint of modern astronomy, the total time for the cycle of conjunctions to go from a particular degree to that same degree again (roughly) is about 795 years, not 960, and the length of stay in one element averages at about one-quarter of that with tremendous variations. The medieval astronomers did not have the correct value for the length of the Jupiter and Saturn cycles.

Medieval astrologers did not use the cycle from actual conjunctions to actual conjunctions, but rather an average or mean cycle. This does not affect the cycle length but it does create a much more orderly progression of degrees from conjunction to conjunction. Figure 16 on page 254 represents this averaged cycle. And when we add to this the fact that the conjunction cycles are centered on the Earth where the planets appear to go backward (retrograde) as well as forward, the actual conjunction positions depart even more from the average. This is especially important with regard to the mutations from element to element. As the conjunction cycles get near the boundaries of signs, the extra irregularities of the real conjunctions may cause conjunctions to occur in the "wrong" element. The table on pages 209–10 shows how this has happened in the last 400 years.

M	Da	Year	Conjunction	Triplicity	
12	18	1603	8Sg19	Fire	
7	16	1623	6Le36	Fire	
2	24	1643	25Pi07	Water	
10	16	1663	12Sg58	Fire	
10	24	1682	19Le09	Fire	
2	9	1683	16Le43	Fire	Single Conjunction
5	18	1683	14Le30	Fire	
5	21	1702	6Ar36	Fire	
1	5	1723	23Sg19	Fire	
8	30	1742	27Le09	Fire	
3	18	1762	12Ar21	Fire	
11	5	1782	28Sg07	Fire	
7	17	1802	5Vi08	Earth	
6	19	1821	24Ar39	Fire	
1	26	1842	8Cp54	Earth	
10	21	1861	18Vi22	Earth	
4	18	1881	1Ta36	Earth	
11	28	1901	14Cp00	Earth	
9	10	1921	26Vi36	Earth	
8	8	1940	14Ta27	Earth	
10	20	1940	12Ta28	Earth	Single Conjunction
2	15	1941	9Ta07	Earth	
2	19	1961	25Cp12	Earth	
12	31	1980	9Li30	Air	
3	4	1981	8Li06	Air	Single Conjunction
7	24	1981	4Li56	Air	
5	28	2000	22Ta43	Earth	
12	21	2020	0Aq29	Air	
10	31	2040	17Li56	Air	

M	Da	Year	Conjunction	Triplicity
4	7	2060	0Ge46	Air
3	15	2080	11Aq52	Air

Abbreviations of Signs

Ar = Aries	Li = Libra
Ta = Taurus	Sc = Scorpio
Ge = Gemini	Sg = Sagittarius
Cn = Cancer	Cp = Capricorn
Le = Leo	Aq = Aquarius
Vi = Virgo	Pi = Pisces

You will notice that sometimes three conjunctions occur within a year. This is caused by the fact that as the Earth goes around the Sun it passes the outer planets in its orbit causing them to look as if they were going backward, much as happens when you pass a slower moving car on the highway. A planet that is farther away from the Earth seems to go backward more slowly that one that is closer. For our purposes, these conjunctions should be counted as single conjunction.

Because of the irregularities in the orbits of the two planets around the Sun, coupled with the fact that we are looking at these conjunctions from an Earth-centered point of view, these factors cause another problem that we would not have if the orbits were (1) perfectly regular, and (2) really around the Earth rather than around the Sun.

In 1603 the conjunctions began to happen in the fire signs but were interrupted by a single water conjunction in 1643. The fire conjunctions then went on until 1802 when we had a conjunction in an earth sign. Then in 1821 it was back in fire again. Not until 1842 did the conjunctions regularly begin to happen in the earth signs. The same thing has happened with the movement of the conjunctions from earth to air in the late twentieth century. After a series of conjunction in earth ending in 1961, we had three conjunctions in air in 1980–81, followed by yet another conjunction in earth in 2000.

How do we know which of these conjunctions is the mutation conjunction? Was the first one from water to fire in 1603 or 1663? From fire to earth was it 1802 or 1842? From earth to air was 1980–81, or will it be 2020? In 1980 many astrologers believed that the mutation conjunction was that triple group of conjunctions in 1980–81. But these same astrologers believed that 1842 was the fire to earth mutation. This is not consistent. I believe that the mutations were in 1663, 1842, and will be in 2020.[5] These are the conjunctions that truly began a series of several conjunctions all in the same triplicity.

Medieval Cycle Charts
The medieval tables of planetary positions used in the 1700s were not accurate enough to give even approximate

---

5. For those who are historically minded here is my evidence. The water conjunctions began in 1425. This is just at the very earliest beginnings of the Renaissance. The Renaissance turned rapidly into the Reformation which in turn culminated in the wars of religion. These when on until the Thirty Years War ended in Europe and the end of the English Civil War with Oliver Cromwell, etc. The year 1662 as the Mutation Conjunction perfectly brackets this entire period with the 1425 conjunction. The choice of 1802 versus 1842 is more difficult. But by 1842 the Industrial Revolution had begun to spread outside of England, and it was not until the period from 1830–48 that the last vestiges of the eighteenth-century way of being with the divine right of kings and all that passing away. My arguments for 2020 as opposed to 1980–81 will be presented below.

times for conjunctions of Jupiter and Saturn. They also could not have computed the time of a conjunction of Mars and Saturn. So how could they do cycle charts type as defined in numbers 1–4 on page 206? Abu Ma'shar is quite clear on this. What they did was to erect charts for the entry of the Sun into Aries (the beginning of spring) that occurs just prior to a conjunction. They used these ingress charts instead of the conjunction charts. What this boils down is that all of Abu Ma'shar's cycle charts except for ones erected for New and Full Moons are charts for the beginning of spring or other season.

Following the medieval criteria, have we had a Great Conjunction that we can point to? Even with all of the irregularities that attend the cycles of Jupiter/Saturn conjunctions, there was a conjunction in 1702 that fit the criteria.[6] All we need to do is to look at the chart for the beginning of spring immediately before the conjunction. The conjunction occurred at approximately 8:55 P.M. Greenwich Mean Time on May 21, 1702. Spring began that year 2:11:40 A.M. GMT on March 21. See Figure 15 on page 253. According to Abu Ma'shar's teachings, that is the chart of the Modern Era and will be relevant for about 795 years, or until 2497. See Modern Era chart, Figure 15 on page 253.

Washington, D.C. and New York Are Power Points

In 1702, New York City was already known as New York, but Washington, D.C., did not exist.[7] Yet the chart for the Modern Era shows dramatically the longitudes of New

---

6. The conjunction in 1702 was at 6 degrees Aries 36 minutes.

York City and Washington, D.C., to be centers of great power for transformation, be it good or bad. Is this a meaningless coincidence?

The United States in 1945

One indication of the possible answer to that question is that Pluto takes about 243 years to make complete cycle of the zodiac. If we add 243 years to 1702 we come up with 1945! And if we look at the ephemeris for that time, we find that in October of 1945, just after the Japanese surrender, Pluto began to transit the Midheaven of the 1702 Modern Era chart, and it continued to cross the Midheaven of Washington and its own position in the 1702 chart through late 1945, 1946, and 1947. These are the years when it became clear that only two nations on Earth were left as superpowers, the USSR and the U.S.A.

The End of USSR Supremacy

And here is another fact to show that this is not a mere coincidence. Pluto began moving rather quickly in the 1970s and 1980s so that by 1988–89 Pluto came to square its position in the 1702 chart for the second time. The year 1989 was the year that the communist world (outside of China) fell apart and the United States emerged as the only superpower.

---

7. It has the zodiacal position of Pluto almost exactly on the Midheaven. The reason for this is that Pluto usually is quite a few degrees above or below the central plane of the zodiac, also known as the ecliptic. Because of the geometry of the celestial sphere any body that is not exactly on the ecliptic will cross the Midheaven at a slightly different time than the point of the zodiac on the ecliptic that is given as its zodiacal position.

But before we leave this we need to make a point. The meridians of New York and Washington are the only meridians in the world were the Pluto of the 1702 is on the Midheaven. To be sure these lines also pass through regions of Canada and South America and it is possible that some of these areas may play a role comparable to the United States' current role in another part of the 1702 Great Conjunction period.

Hanoi and Vietnam

There is one last interesting point. The capital city of Hanoi in Asia is exactly opposite in longitude to New York. Hanoi is the only capital city of a nation which has defeated the United States in a war. Pluto is on the I.C of the 1702 (in the location of Hanoi), which is exactly opposite the Midheaven location in New York and Washington.

Modern Era Chart Related to the Present

The transits of the attack to the 1702 chart are quite striking. Most important is that Pluto, at the time of the attack on September 11, is exactly trine (120 degrees) to the Pluto/Midheaven combination of the 1702 chart. As we have already seen, Pluto transits to the Pluto of the 1702 have been most important in past history.

By the time of the counterattack on October 7, 2001, the Sun, Mars, and Jupiter had formed a T-square.[8] Based on that aspect alone I expected the counterattack to begin at about that time because this combination was very close to the Suns of both the United States (1776) chart, and George W. Bush's chart. What I did not know, until I began

---

8. Mars was opposite Jupiter and the Sun squared them both.

doing to research for this article, was that the T-square was very close to the Uranus of the 1702 chart which is in Ninth House of that chart, indicating something to do with foreign nations. Mars/Jupiter means fortunate or productive actions being taken. The Sun simply adds power to it and helps to time the day of the event. Uranus means a sudden or disturbing event.

Caution Is Needed

This combination of Mar/Jupiter/Sun does indicate a tendency to overdo things; to take risks that are too large. The government has acted with restraint thus far, but it has not defined the scope of what it intends to achieve as of this writing (October 10, 2001) and this could lead to the negative manifestations of this combination.

Forewarning

Before we leave the 1702 chart, there is one more important thing to mention. We have already seen that the Pluto trine Pluto of the 1702 chart is important—attacks on United States in 2001. But it tells us something more specific. Trines usually suggest productive outcomes if one chooses to take action during them, and we *have* taken action. But simply "taking care" of bin Laden and company is not a long-range enough answer. It doesn't alter the basic problem of terrorism. While we are right to condemn the senseless slaughter of thousands of innocents, we had best change the way we do business in foreign nations.

The last trine of Pluto (in 1702 chart) to transiting Pluto was in the 1830s (see footnote 5 on page 211). This was followed by Pluto square Pluto aspect in 1863 to 1866 (Civil War period). In the 1830s various compromises were tried between the slave states and the free states regarding slavery. Nothing was accomplished except to make both sides more intransigent. The result was that the following square was most brutal period of the Civil War.

Next Difficult Time in United States History

From now the next difficult combination of Pluto to the 1702 Pluto is the opposition of the late 2070s. I do not expect to see this time, but what we do now will have a tremendous result in about that time. If we do well, then that will not be a bad time. If we do not, then there will be a tremendous breakdown, far greater than the Civil War for our nation.

The Mutation Conjunction of 1842

The Mutation Conjunction of 1842 occurred at 1:13 A.M. EST January 26, 1842. The previous beginning spring began at 1:27:45 P.M. EST on March 20, 1841. It is remarkable that, as in the 1702 chart, the zodiacal position of the planet Pluto is again zodiacally on the Midheaven in Washington, D.C.! The actual planetary body of Pluto as a point was on the Midheaven in Boston, Massachusetts. The two types of Pluto/Midheaven line bracket the northeast of the United States. This region was about to undergo an unprecedented expansion of power and influence. (Remember that this chart has influence and signification from 1841 until the spring of 2020.) This Pluto is in a very close trine (120 degree angle) to Jupiter. The combination of

Jupiter and Pluto indicates powerful growth, fortunate transformations, and regeneration. This clearly describes the tremendous growth of power and prestige that was to take place in the following mutation cycle in the northeast United States.

How does this chart relate to the events of September and October? This chart does not interact as strongly with the recent planetary positions as the 1702 chart but there are a couple of indications worth mentioning. First of all, the Mars of September 11, 2001, is conjunct the Saturn of the 1841 chart. That Saturn is in the Sixth House of the 1841 chart. Many astrologers maintain that house gives indications for the military services, "service" being a Sixth House word. Mars in the September 11 chart on that degree can easily be read as indicating an event that calls the services into action. Second, Neptune on September 11 is making a square to the Mars in Scorpio of the 1841 chart, which is in the Fourth House of real property and buildings. This clearly indicates some kind of Mars incident (fire, explosions, etc.) happening in such a way as to be weakening. It could also indicate something like "sneak attack."

The Chart of the Mars/Saturn Cycle in 1974

According to Abu Ma'shar, the thirty-years Mars/Saturn cycle chart is the chart for the beginning of spring prior to the conjunction of Mars and Saturn in the sign Cancer, as defined in number three in the beginning of this article. This happened on April 20, 1974, at 9:52:15 A.M. EDT. The conjunction itself was at 0 degrees and 8 minutes of Cancer.

Although we are relying on the preceding spring charts following Abu Ma'shar, this chart is interesting in itself for two reasons.

First, the conjunction occurred at the beginning of a cardinal sign,[9] which is generally considered to be an especially significant position.

Second, the previous spring began at 8:06:46 P.M. EDT[10] March 20, 1974.

The Mars/Saturn cycle chart was believed to be a chart mostly of mayhem and disaster since it was the chart of the coming together of the two malefics, Mars, "the lesser malefic," and Saturn, "the greater malefic." While we must make allowances for the tendency of traditional writers in astrology to state things in horrendous terms, the following passage from William Ramesey, a seventeen-century writer does not seem too severe for the present circumstances.

> In like manner the *Conjunction* of *Saturn* and *Mars* in the first degree or term of *Cancer*, is the forerunner of much evill, [yet are the two former preferred before it][11] viz. Terrible wars, slaughters, depopulations and alterations of Government; and the destruction of Kingdoms, fire and sword, famine and pestilence,

---

9. The cardinal signs are the ones that begin each season for which we erect ingress charts. They are Aries, Cancer, Libra, and Capricorn.

10. That was a year of energy shortages and Daylight Saving Time was used all year.

11. This refers to the two previous types of cycle chart from Jupiter and Saturn described just above.

etc.[12] [Punctuation, spelling, and typography as in the original.]

This chart has Pluto rising but not exactly on the Ascendant in Washington; also Uranus is in the First House. But perhaps its most intriguing feature is Mars in Gemini in the Ninth House of foreign places and long-distance journeys, which is opposed by Neptune in the Third House of short journeys. The significance of this will become clearer below. But the basic symbolism indicates difficulties in long-distance transportation and Mars/Neptune combinations can have to do with fanatical actions motivated by religion. And let us keep in mind that this chart not only precedes the advent of difficulties from Islamic extremists, it also precedes the rise of religious extremism in this country.

Now about that Mars/Neptune opposition in the 1974 chart, the position of Mars at 12 degrees Gemini 12 minutes is close to Saturn in the September 11 chart, and even closer to the opposition of the Pluto in that chart at 12 degrees and 38 minutes of Sagittarius. Also the Neptune in the 1974 chart is very close to being opposed to the Uranus in the July 4, 1776 chart. In the version of that chart that I use Uranus is in the Seventh House of open enemies. Neptune again indicates something covert or hidden.

The Jupiter/Saturn Conjunction of 2000

The next level of conjunction is the Jupiter/Saturn cycle in which an event occurs. This is indicated by the spring

---

12. William Ramesey, *Astrologia Restaurata, or Astrologie Restored* (London: 1653, facsimile Ascella Publications), 328.

ingress chart that precedes it. The conjunction occurred on May 28, 2000, so we go to the previous spring which began at 2:35:37 A.M. EST March 20, 2000. This chart features Jupiter on the I.C. in Washington, D.C. in a close square (90 degrees) to Neptune in the Second House. This ingress occurred just as the stock market had peaked and was in a wave of speculative frenzy. This is a classic Jupiter/Neptune phenomenon. Neptune and Uranus, both in the Second House of money and finance, were warnings that things were getting shaky on the economic front. Neptune being 90 degrees from the I.C. could also be read as warning about something that might happen to real property and buildings. However, this is said with the advantage of hindsight. It is only with my recent small success in using these ingress charts to forecast events that I have begun to discover just how useful they can be.[13]

The main connection between this chart and the chart of the events of September and October is that the Ascendant of this chart is close to opposition of the July 4, 1776, Sun, which is also President Bush's Sun. But even more significant is the fact that the Mars/Jupiter/Sun T-square referred to above that formed around the time of our counterattack was closely tied to the Ascendant and Descendant of this chart. Mars was conjunct the Ascendant of this chart, Jupiter the Descendant, and the Sun was square both. When T-squares happen on important points in the chart of a cycle, it indicates something significant is about to happen in that cycle.

---

13. Robert Hand, "A Crisis of Power: Saturn and Pluto Face Off," in *The Mountain Astrologer*, August/September 2001.

The Seasonal Charts for 2001

There are two charts that I would normally choose to look at for a date such as September 11, 2001: the spring chart, which to some extent governs the entire year; and the summer chart, which is the last season beginning before the attacks. The beginning of spring in 2001 occurred at 8:30:02 A.M. EST March 20. This chart has Saturn rising close to the Ascendant. This is an indication of the people of the nation (First House) being concerned with heavy and weighty matters. This could have simply indicated concern with economy. However, we have Jupiter in the Second House of money, which normally would be a good sign for the economy. However, Jupiter is in Gemini, the sign of its detriment,[14] which means that its effects are not as useful as usual. And Mercury the planet that rules[15] the Second House is in Pisces, which is both the sign of its detriment and its fall.[16] They are also in close square (90 degree angle) to each other.

The other notable items in this chart are Neptune near the Midheaven with the Moon, which indicates doubt and uncertainty in the government—especially with regard to the people (the Moon and the First House both indicate

---

14. The sign of detriment is the sign opposite to the sign that a planet rules or is said to have the closest connection with. Jupiter "rules" Sagittarius so it is in detriment in Gemini the opposite sign.

15. See previous note.

16. Fall occurs when a planet is in the sign opposite the sign said to be its exaltation. Exaltation is slightly less powerful than sign rulership of the usual kind, but it is powerful. Mercury rules and is exalted in the same sign, the only planet for which that is true. Therefore, it is in both fall in detriment in Pisces the opposite sign.

the people). But in retrospect the most ominous thing in the chart is the conjunction of Mars and Pluto in the Eighth House. This is not something that I could have anticipated in advance. One does not anticipate the inconceivable and September 11 was inconceivable. This is a clear indication of mass death and destruction in the following year. Could it have meant something else? Certainly! And that is what I assumed it would be. All astrological indications occur in an historical context. We did not know last spring what the historical context was about to be. Uranus in the Tenth House square to Ascendant and to Saturn in the First House also shows that there might be great agitation of the people. Incidentally, this Saturn was exactly conjunct the Ascendant in New York City.

The beginning of summer occurred at 3:36:52 A.M. EDT June 21, 2001. This chart features Neptune very close to the Midheaven. It actually was on the Midheaven in New York City, marking New York as the likely location of a sneak (Neptune) attack. The other main peculiarity of this chart is that there is just about to be a New Moon and that New Moon is an eclipse. I mentioned earlier that the actual position of the Mars/Saturn conjunction in 1974 was 0 degrees and 8 minutes of Cancer. The eclipse just after the summer ingress occurred at 0 degrees and 10 minutes of Cancer. That is a *two-minute* difference! Eclipses are not part of the classic Abu Ma'shar system, but since ancient times they have always been part of the general scheme of mundane forecasting. This eclipse indicates that a major manifestation of the Mars/Saturn conjunction symbolism from 1974 was about to take place.

The New and Full Moons Preceding

Now we are down to the shortest-term cycle charts the New and Full Moons. The New Moon occurred at 10:54 P.M. EDT August 18, 2001. It is not immediately obvious that it is a significant chart, but an ominous sign in light of later events is that the Saturn/Pluto opposition of 2001–02 is between the Second (money) and Eighth (death) Houses. These are in turn both squared by Mercury in the Fifth House, which rules speculation and stock markets. This chart is clearly not favorable for the markets, and something to do with deaths is indicated.

The Full Moon was at 5:40:36 P.M. EDT September 2, 2001. This chart is much more ominous than the New Moon. It would be hard to over look its significance. The Full Moon is between the Sun at 10 degrees and 28 minutes of Virgo and the Moon in the same position in Pisces, the Sun being in the Eighth House of death and the Moon in Second House of money. They are in square (90 degrees) to Saturn at 14 degrees and 27 minutes Gemini in the Fifth House (speculation and stock markets) and Pluto at 12 degrees and 34 minutes of Sagittarius in the Eleventh House of groups, organizations, corporations, etc. This combination is what is called a Grand Square where we have planets at the four corners of a square figure and two oppositions running down the middle of the square figure. This is quite a difficult combination.

Could anyone have forecast this on the basis of this chart alone? Of course not! It is only when we assemble the weight of all of the indications that we can see, at least in retrospect, what was coming. I also want to say at this point that the method that I have described here is not generally in use by modern astrologers, that is, this systematic examination of cycle charts and ingresses running down from the Great Conjunction, to the Mutation Conjunction, the Mars/Saturn cycle, etc.

These last elements of the system, the immediately preceding spring, summer, New Moon, and Full Moon charts, along with the eclipse chart, are the only ones that can time the event by themselves to any degree. The longer-range charts must at some level single out the places involved in the events by putting planets on the Ascendant, Midheaven, Descendant, or I.C., or through comparison to the planets of the time period indicated by the shorter term cycle charts. Could I have found the events of Sept. 11, 2001, doing all of that? Not precisely, but I could have and did find the approximate date of this entire matter, and I also believe that the chart of our counterattack could also be approximately seen.[17]

Conclusion

So here we have it. A method of historical analysis developed in the Middle Ages, or earlier,[18] that sheds a great deal

---

17. But I did not see anything like the severity of what happened because I could not have conceived of it.

18. I say "earlier" because the documentation of the history of astrology in pre-Islamic Persia was destroyed by the Arabs when they conquered the Persian Empire. But the tradition was not destroyed. It is related to, but somewhat different from, the tradition of the Greek writers in the late Roman era. But when we see that tradition in Abu Ma'shar, it is fully developed and clearly the result a long period if not centuries of development.

of light on the events of the present. It is clear that what we do here will have tremendous impact on the future. Let us hope we are guided by more than the narrow self-interest of the past. If we want the Islamic world to accept us as their brothers and sisters, we must treat them as such, recognizing that at this point there are elements in that world that would never accept us no matter what we did. We must shed the last vestiges of colonialism and assist where possible their coming into the modern world completely, and yet allow them to do on their own terms and maintaining their own civilization. We must remember that the entire methodology used in this article is the creation of that culture. Abu Ma'shar was an ethnic Iranian and he wrote in Arabic and Middle Persian. He and others taught this to our ancestors.

Conclusion

STEPHANIE CLEMENT

Civilization Under Attack—this is a bold title for any book. Throughout the chapters of this book we have demonstrated the astrological realities of the September 11, 2001, attack on the World Trade Center and Washington, D.C. In addition, we have provided historical information about the nations and the personalities involved in the current struggle against terrorism. We have shown how the damage from these incidents will reverberate in the military, political, economic, and human arenas. September 11 marks the end of business as usual.

This date also marks the beginning of something new. We could call it the beginning of the externalization of consciousness. Before this date most of us went about our business, thinking our own thoughts, pursuing our own careers, and relating to our own families. We made use of the elements of globalization, but we didn't think about them all that much. Some of the major elements are these:

1. A global economy, within which we buy and use products from all over the world. This global economy is not yet the sophisticated entity that it can become, with a global infrastructure to support a single currency. We do have the capacity to travel around the world in twenty-four hours. And we are developing global awareness that extends from conservation of the Amazon rain forest to how to manage oil spills in Alaska.

2. An international language, business English has always integrated words from other languages, such as sputnik, fatwah, watusi, and I Ching. Where English won't work, we have computers to translate languages and facilitate communication across borders.

3. A global information network, the Internet provides instant communication and a means to share and store information.

All of this was present in our world before September 11, 2001. What happened on that date was the presentation—birth—of the unification of individual consciousness into global consciousness. What the death of John Kennedy was for the United States, what the death of Princess Diana was for Great Britain, what the death of Mother Teresa was for India, this terrorist act was for the entire world. Within moments, and certainly over the few days following September 11, the world came together as one mind, raising the consciousness of the planet forever.

Carl Weschcke, president of Llewellyn Worldwide, put it this way:

"Never before in history had it been possible, but with this event human consciousness was united—not at a high spiritual level 'where we are all one' but right here in our mental bodies. At this moment, I believe we came together in a mental collective outside our physical bodies. It is similar to the emotional experience of coming together in a circle dance or common prayer—but this was at the mind level on a dimension that was truly global."

Relating Global Consciousness to Astrology

The chart for the September 11 attack has been discussed throughout this book. I want to say a few more things about it from the perspective of the emerging global mind.

The Sun in this chart is in the sign of Virgo. This sign exemplifies the strength to be found in cooperation. You have read about the intense cooperative effort of the terrorists in planning and executing their mission, and of rescue workers who searched for survivors. The same intensity can attend the development of global consciousness. Scientific evidence is emerging concerning this very point.

The Global Consciousness Project at Princeton University has created a network of "eggs," placed around the world to generate random data continuously. The terrorist attack is reflected in the data in remarkable ways.[1] In graphs

---

1. "Terrorist Disaster, September 11, 2001," at http://noosphere.pinceton.edu, in a link from Global Consciousness Project.

reflecting the data from the random generators, "the slope of the graph beginning just before the first crash and continuing for nearly three days, to the end of the [September 13], is extreme." The odds are estimated to be "on the order of 1 in 1000." Dean Radin states, "These effects are the most strikingly persuasive evidence I've seen so far that mass-mind attention/intention affects the physical world, perhaps because this event has also been the most horrific."

The data reflected the tremendous outpouring of feeling in the days following the disaster, as rescuers worked frantically to find people known to be alive beneath the collapsed buildings, and leading up to collective spiritual moments on the of September 14. "One way to think of these startling correlations is to accept the possibility that the instruments have captured the reaction of a global consciousness beginning to form. The network was built to do just that: to see whether we could gather evidence of a communal, shared mind in which we are participants even if we don't know it."

What further information can we gather about this global consciousness? The Moon in the chart erected for the first attack on the World Trade Center is in the late degrees of Gemini. This sign reflects the "relationships with the persons of the environment and with family. Exchange of thoughts."[2] Placed in the Ninth House, the sector of the chart astrologers relate to both higher philosophy and to airline travel, foreign countries and foreign trade, in gen-

---

2. Reinhold Ebertin, *The Combination of Stellar Influences* (Ebertin Verlag, 1972), 41.

eral, the Gemini Moon suggests the very sort of mind-melding communication reflected in the Princeton study.

It also reflects something even more intriguing. The astrology of events suggests that when the Moon is in the very late degrees of a sign, past the formation of aspects to any of the planets before it enters the next sign, we should consider the word "nothing" as an indication of the outcome. Earlier in the book I stated that in my opinion, nothing could have been done to prevent the terrorist attacks.

Mercury rising in this chart points to communication and cooperation as the essence of the event. The terrorist attack stands in starkest contrast to the evidence of an emerging planetary awareness. I can't think of a more extreme polarization of energy—massive destruction motivated by fundamentalist religious belief on the one hand, and profound integration and spiritual wisdom on the other.

The Moon does make one aspect before it leaves Gemini and enters the sign of Cancer, and that is to parallel Jupiter. This is not a conjunction. What it means is that the Moon and Jupiter are at the same declination. Declination is a measurement of how far planets are from the ecliptic—the path of the Earth around the Sun. The parallel is considered to be very fortunate, especially when Jupiter is involved. What is more, the Moon and Jupiter are both moving toward this parallel. The parallel is "always good, bringing two significators [planets] together to conclude

---

3. Ivy Goldstein-Jacobson, *Simplified Horary Astrology* (Ivy M. Goldstein-Jacobson, 1970), 79.

the matter."[3] The full outcome "will be a long in coming to pass," but "it is as good as done now."[4] These statements pertain to the terrorist attacks, and they also pertain to the birth of global consciousness. Such a consciousness is a done deal. In fact it may have existed for a long time, and what has happened is only the "birth" of our awareness of it as a reality. I am intrigued by the fact that the Moon was in the exact same degree of longitude as the Pole Star—Polaris—on September 11 at the time of the first crash. The Moon is showing us our direction as we move into the future.

Now the question arises: What shall we do with this global consciousness? We stand at the threshold of an evolutionary leap. Robert Hand, in his article "Great Conjunctions," suggests that we are in a lull between the end of an earth element cycle and the beginning of an air element cycle. We can choose between 1981 and 2020 as the dates for the definitive beginning of the new cycle, and Hand makes a strong argument for the 2020 date. The air element is totally consistent with the concept of the externalization of consciousness. No longer must we muddle through with the ideas we individually generate. We can use the power of mind to meld ideas from people around the planet. We can tackle problems that seemed beyond our capacity before.

I quote Carl Weschcke again: "We can recognize the errors of the past that have led up to this tragedy (I include all that happened and is happening—New York, Palestine, Afghanistan, etc.), but we can't fix the past. We can only

---

4. Ibid.

look to the future we desire and try to understand how to get there; then make the decisions to act with intelligence. The key is the event itself: So long as it remains a strong emotional force, we can use it to bring people back into the experience of the world mind. With that, we reinforce global consciousness."

Contributors

BERNIE ASHMAN has a degree in political science with a focus on international politics. In addition to his career as a social worker, he has been a practicing astrologer for over twenty-five years, and he is the author of several books, including *Astrological Games People Play* (ACS Publications), *Roadmap to Your Future* (Reprinted by AFA), *SignMates* (Llewellyn), and he has a fourth book under contract with Llewellyn.

STEPHANIE JEAN CLEMENT, PH.D., a professional astrologer for over twenty-five years, is a board member of the American Federation of Astrologers and a member of the faculty of Kepler College, the only United States college or university to offer degrees in astrology. She has a Ph.D. in Transpersonal Psychology and has written seven books on astrology and one about dreams.

DAVID CROOK has actively studied the I Ching, Taoism, metaphysics, and astrology for twenty years. He is also a working visual artist with a Masters of Fine Arts degree from the San Francisco Art Institute. For the last two years, he has focused on the study of mundane astrology, while continuing to consult with private clients.

ROBERT HAND has been studying astrology and the history of astrology for over thirty years. One of the foremost astrologers in the world today, his particular areas of expertise are in classical medieval astrology and modern theory. He is the founder and director of ARHAT, an archive and publishing house for astrological research and historical texts. He is the author of such classic texts as *Planets in Transit* and *Essays in Astrology*.

JONATHAN KEYES, B.S., is an astrologer, herbalist, and plant spirit medicine practitioner. His is a writer for StarIQ.com, and his writing has appeared in *The Mountain Astrologer*. Jon has an astrology and health article in Llewellyn's 2002 *Sun Sign Book*, and his forthcoming book, *Mirror to the Sky: A Guide to Astrological Healing*, will be published by Llewellyn in 2002.

KRIS BRANDT RISKE is a certified professional member of the American Federation of Astrologers. In addition to consulting with clients, she edits astrology books and her articles have been published in *Dell Horoscope* and *Today's Astrologer*. She specializes in relationships, romance, and forecasting. She is the author of *Astrometeorology: Planetary Power in Weather Forecasting*. Her forecasts appear in Llewellyn's *Moon Sign Book* and the *National Examiner*.

GEORGIA STATHIS has been a full-time professional astrologer since 1977. Her background in business, including investments, real estate, public relations, advertising, and marketing, has been a basis for her private work as an astrologer for companies and individuals. A first-generation Greek-American whose cultures' roots are in myth, story, and trade, Stathis is a coauthor of *Financial Astrology for the 1990's* and is the author and publisher of *Starcycles Calendar* appointment books.

Bibliography

Dodson, Carolyn. *Horoscopes of the U.S. and Cities.* (San Diego: ACS Publications, 1985).

Lewis, Jim and Ariel Guttman. *The Astro*Carto*Graphy Book of Maps.* (St. Paul: Llewellyn, 1989).

Shawvan, James. "The Red Planet and the White House: Mars in the Presidency of George W. Bush." *The Mountain Astrologer*, April/May 2001.

Hand, Robert. "A Crisis of Power: Saturn and Pluto Face Off." *The Mountain Astrologer*, August/September, 2001.

Ebertin, Reinhold. *Combination of Stellar Influences.* (Tempe: AFA Publications, 1972).

Hannon, Geraldine Hatch. *Sacred Space.* (Ithaca: Firebrand, 1990).

McNeill, William H. *Plagues and People.* (Garden City: Anchor Books, 1976).

Hone, Margaret. *The Modern Text-Book of Astrology.* (London: Fowler, 1951).

Gauquelin, Michel. *Planetary Heredity.* Reprinted in the U.S. (San Diego: ACS Publications, 1988).

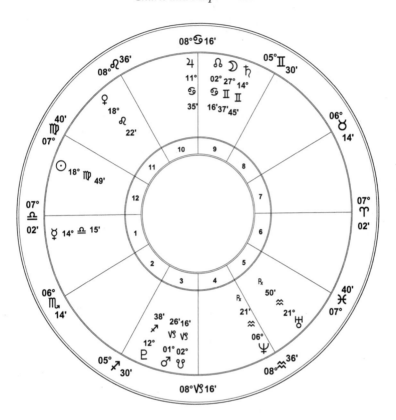

FIGURE 1
Departure time Flight 175
September 11, 2001,
Boston, Massachusetts 7:58 A.M. EDT.

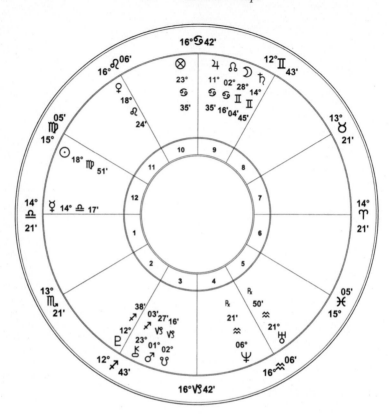

FIGURE 2
First plane crashes into World Trade Center
September 11, 2001,
Manhattan, New York, 8:46 A.M. EDT.

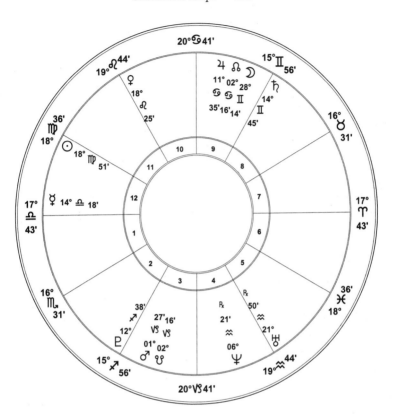

FIGURE 3
Second plane crashes into World Trade Center
September 11, 2001,
Manhattan, New York, 9:03 A.M. EDT.

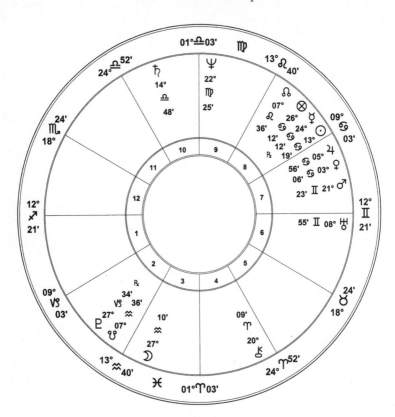

FIGURE 4
United States chart
July 4, 1776,
Philadelphia, Pennsylvania 5:10 P.M. LMT.

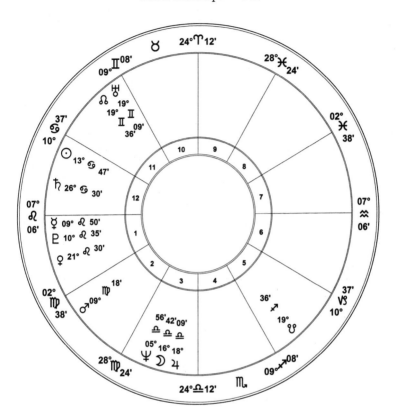

FIGURE 5
George W. Bush
July 6, 1945, New Haven, Connecticut,
7:26 A.M. EWT.

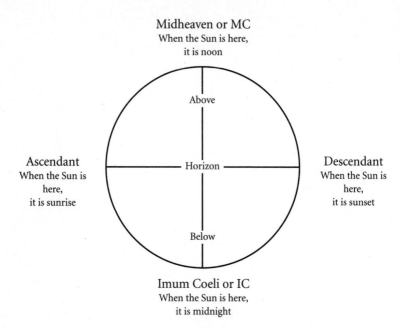

Midheaven or MC
When the Sun is here,
it is noon

Above

Ascendant
When the Sun is
here,
it is sunrise

Horizon

Descendant
When the Sun is
here,
it is sunset

Below

Imum Coeli or IC
When the Sun is here,
it is midnight

FIGURE 6
Circle with angles
The location of the Angles in an astrological chart.

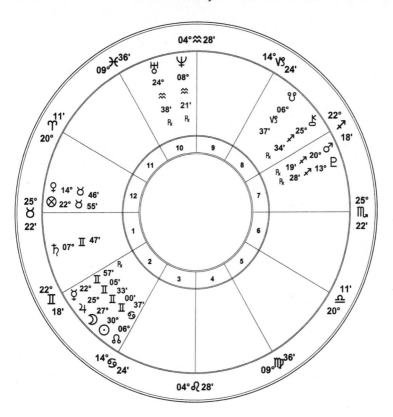

FIGURE 7
Summer Ingress June 2001
June 21, 2001, Washington, D.C., 3:37 A.M. EDT.

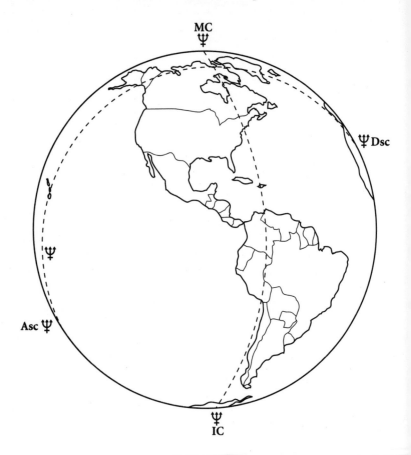

FIGURE 8
June Ingress
Neptune astromap lines for the Summer 2001
Ingress projected onto a globe.

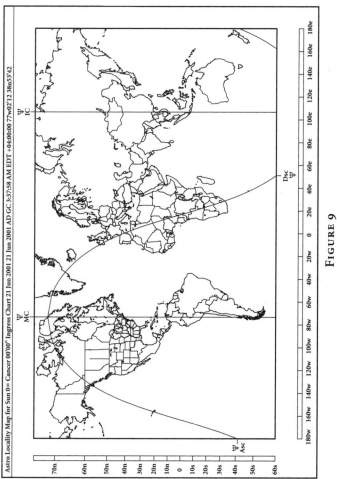

FIGURE 9
Neptune world map
Neptune astromap lines for the Summer 2001 Ingress projected onto a world map.

AstroMaps generated by the Janus astrology software

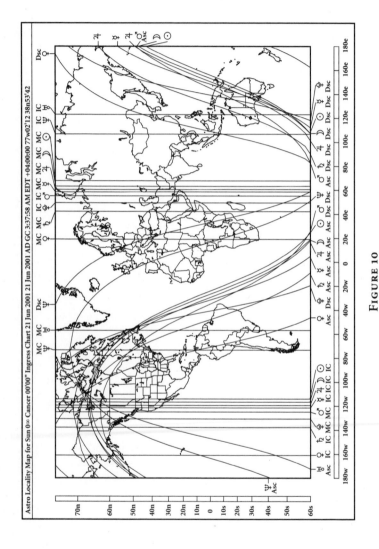

FIGURE 10
Full world map
Full set of astromap lines for the Summer 2001 Ingress projected onto a world map.

AstroMaps generated by the Janus astrology software

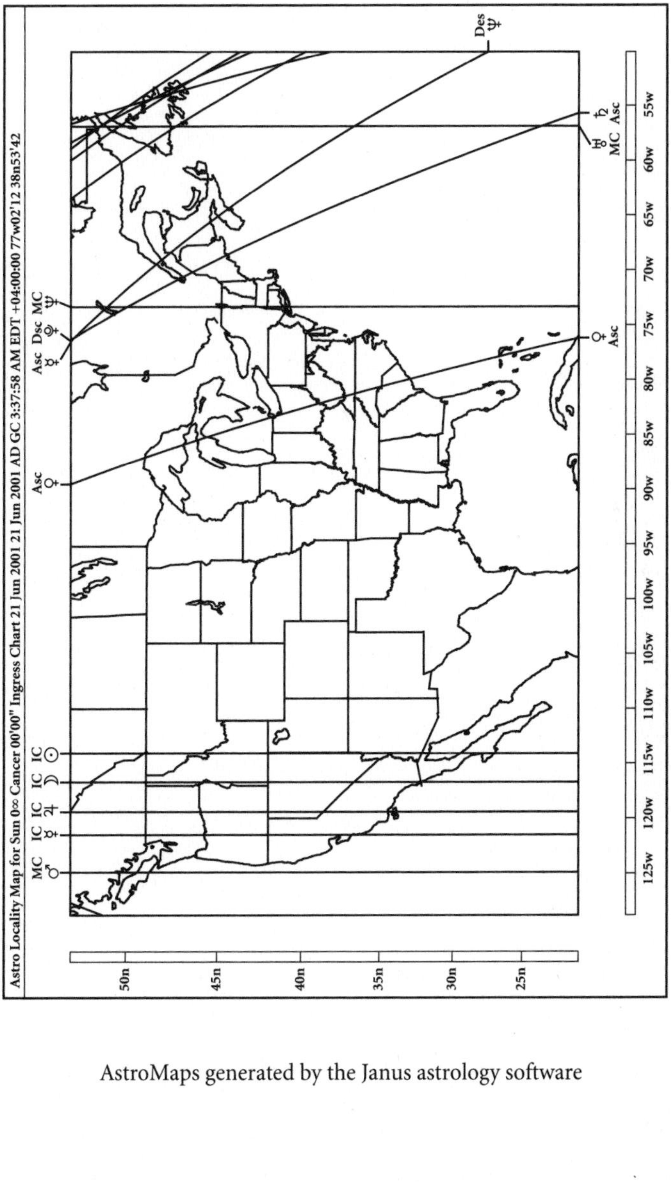

FIGURE 11

Map of United States

Full set of astromap lines for the Summer 2001 Ingress projected onto a map of the United States.

AstroMaps generated by the Janus astrology software

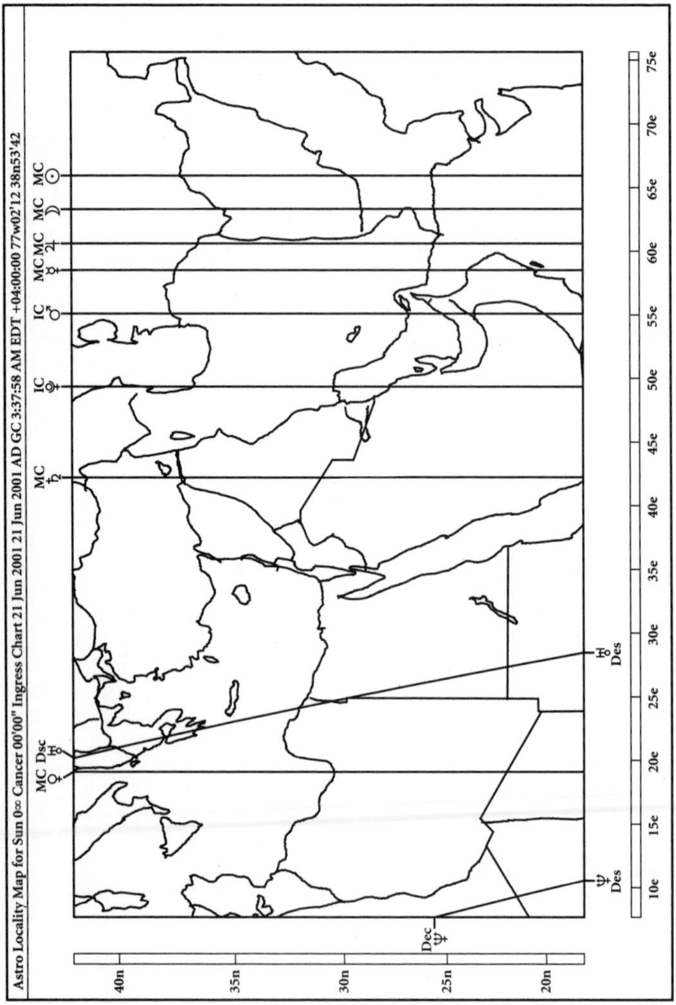

FIGURE 12

Map of Middle East

Full set of astromap lines for the Summer 2001 Ingress projected onto a map of the Middle East.

AstroMaps generated by the Janus astrology software

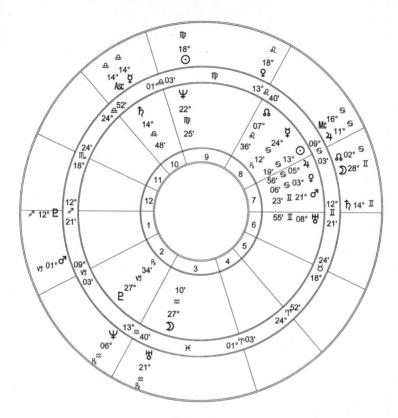

FIGURE 13
Biwheel chart of the United States and first plane crash
at 8:46 A.M. EDT.

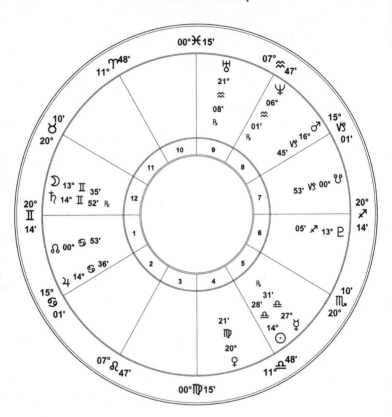

FIGURE 14
United States counterattack
October 7, 2001, 8:57 P.M. AFG.

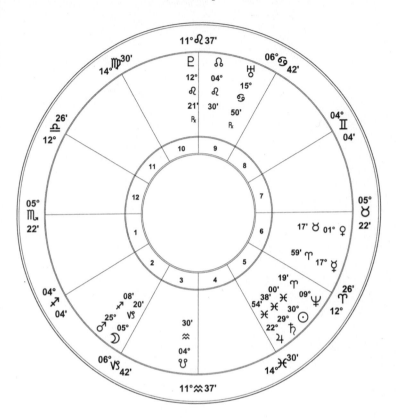

FIGURE 15
Modern Era, March, 21, 1702
Washington, D.C., 2:11 A.M. GMT

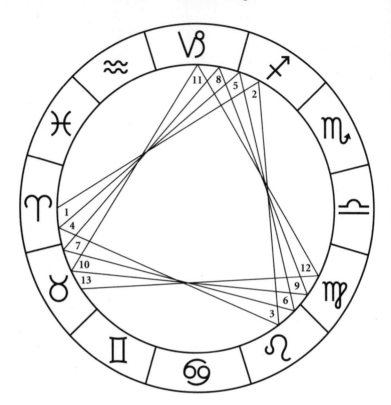

FIGURE 16
Illustration of the Jupiter/Saturn cycle
Illustration of the gradual movement of Jupiter/Saturn
conjunctions through the signs.

This list of chart data is in addition to illustrations shown here. Many thanks to Lois Rodden and Mark McDonough of Astrodatabank for data from their collection.   Other data is self-evident (ingresses), or was found through research on the Internet.

1. Pentagon hit by plane	September 11, 2001, Washington, D.C., 9:43 A.M.
2. Part of Pentagon collapses	10:01 A.M.
3. First World Trade Center tower collapses	10:05 A.M.
4. United Flight 93 crashes in Pennsylvania	10:10 A.M.
5. Second World Trade Center tower collapses	10:28 A.M.
6. Previous World Trade Center bombing	February 26, 1993, 12:18 P.M. EST, 40N43, 74W00
7. Afghanistan Taliban occupation	April 25, 1992, Kabul, Afghanistan, 2:22 P.M. AFST
8. White House cornerstone	October 31, 1792, Washington, D.C.
9. Capitol cornerstone	September 18, 1793, Washington, D.C.
10. Pentagon first occupied	April 29, 1942, 10:30 A.M. EWT 38N54, 77W02—ACS book (38N52, 77W03— Win*Star Plus / ACS data)
11. Pentagon construction began	September 11, 1941
12. Colin Powell	April 5, 1937, noon, New York, New York
13. Secretary Of Defense Rumsfeld	July 9, 1932, 5:40 P.M., Chicago, Illinois

14. NASDAQ first trades	February 8, 1971, 10:00 A.M. EST, New York, New York
15. NYSE—first stock market	May 17, 1792, noon, New York, New York
16. NYSE constitution and name	March 8, 1817
17. Manhattan—first municipal government	February 12, 1653, noon, New Amsterdam, New York
18. New York City consolidates boroughs	January 1, 1898, 12:01 A.M., 40n46, 73W59
19. State of Israel	May 14, 1948, 4:37 P.M. EET, 34E46, 32N04,-2L00 time zone
20. Tony Blair	May 6, 1953, 6:10 A.M. BST, Edinburgh, Scotland
21. Vladimir Putin	October 7, 1952, 9:30 A.M. BAT, St. Petersburg, Russia 30E15, 59N55
22. Spring Ingress 1702	March 21, 1702, 2:11:40 A.M. GMT
23. Ingress September 2001	September 22, 2001, 7:04 P.M. EDT
24. Ingress December 2001	December 21, 2001, 2:23 P.M. EST
25. Ingress March 2002	March 20, 2002, 2:26 P.M. EST
26. Ingress June 2002	June 21, 2002, 9:24 P.M. EDT
27. Ingress September 2002	September 23, 2002, 23:55 A.M. EDT
28. Dick Cheney	January 30, 1941, 7:30 P.M. CST, Lincoln, NE